Ontologies, Taxonomies and Thesauri in Systems Science and Systematics

CHANDOS
INFORMATION PROFESSIONAL SERIES

Series Editor: Ruth Rikowski
(email: Rikowskigr@aol.com)

Chandos' new series of books are aimed at the busy information professional. They have been specially commissioned to provide the reader with an authoritative view of current thinking. They are designed to provide easy-to-read and (most importantly) practical coverage of topics that are of interest to librarians and other information professionals. If you would like a full listing of current and forthcoming titles, please visit our web site www.chandospublishing.com or email info@chandospublishing.com or telephone +44 (0) 1223 891358.

New authors: we are always pleased to receive ideas for new titles; if you would like to write a book for Chandos, please contact Dr Glyn Jones on email gjones@chandospublishing.com or telephone number +44 (0) 1993 848726.

Bulk orders: some organisations buy a number of copies of our books. If you are interested in doing this, we would be pleased to discuss a discount. Please email info@chandospublishing.com or telephone +44 (0) 1223 891358.

Ontologies, Taxonomies and Thesauri in Systems Science and Systematics

EMILIA CURRÁS

CHANDOS
PUBLISHING

Oxford · Cambridge · New Delhi

Chandos Publishing
TBAC Business Centre
Avenue 4
Station Lane
Witney
Oxford OX28 4BN
UK
Tel: +44 (0) 1993 848726
Email: info@chandospublishing.com
www.chandospublishing.com

Chandos Publishing is an imprint of Woodhead Publishing Limited

Woodhead Publishing Limited
Abington Hall
Granta Park
Great Abington
Cambridge CB21 6AH
UK
www.woodheadpublishing.com

First published in 2010

ISBN:
978 1 84334 612 8

© E. Currás, 2010

Typeset by Domex e-Data Pvt. Ltd.
Printed in the UK and USA.

In the Unit of Wisdom,

where Philosophy joins Science

and the borders become fuzzy,

we obtain, by the conjunction of Ontologies, Taxonomies

and Systems Science and Systematics,

the order which brings us to a greater angle of abstraction

and compression,

towards the future progress,

always by the path of Information Technology.

E.C.

Translator
Carmen Campuzano

Thanks

Sincere thanks to Marta Requena and Fanny Albarracín
for their help in the preparation of the manuscript.

Contents

List of figures

Foreword

To those who work outside the boundaries of librarianship, documentation and technical information service provision, the word 'thesaurus' is most likely to conjure up the name Roget, whose *Thesaurus of English Words and Phrases* was first published in 1852. This work, which has been published in many editions and languages since the nineteenth century, ingeniously arranges synonyms and near synonyms in clusters under head-words, which themselves are arranged in near and universal classification, the whole supported by an alphabetical index to all the words in the volume.

In its more modern structure, adding more semantic relationships and additional information, it is still used as a tool in information retrieval, but increasingly as a structured vocabulary to support a range of tools from taxonomies to file plans for records management. Hence the thesaurus which came into being in the early 1960s and has been used ever since in a wide range of systems both manual and computerised has not only survived but evolved. A large number of thesauri have been compiled in most every subject imaginable, and are still being compiled today.

The first books and standards on thesaurus construction, written in the 1970s, were addressed to professional information workers, many of whom had at least some understanding of the principles of classification but needed now to understand how to build tools with greater specificity and to effectively use the retrieval power offered by post-coordinate systems. Then came the revolution: distributed systems, full-text searching using a new breed of search engines, culminating in the arrival of the World Wide Web – that gargantuan, anarchic database that is said to double in size every 11 hours. At one time, it seemed that the professional information intermediary was an endangered species, as information providers and software vendors alike fought to persuade anybody with a personal computer that searching was easy. We now know two things. First, today's 'knowledge workers' are drowning in a sea of information; even large corporations have several million items on their intranets, often very poorly organised. The second reality that is observed is that the great majority of people do not know how to carry out effective searches. One study of a billion accesses of the Altavista search site has shown that one in five people failed to enter a term into the search box at all, one in four entered a single term, and one in four entered a two-word phrase. Eighty per cent of those searching for information did not use any Boolean operators in this study.

Given these two facts, it becomes obvious that never before are we in such need of new and better approaches to information retrieval, including a wider range of tools to satisfy the different needs of a huge and disparate audience. One of these is the 'taxonomy' which, though it initially became something of a buzzword, has now become a standard tool on many websites, offering easier searching and browsing through systems of connected menus. Unfortunately, the literature describing taxonomy compilation is patchy, though the emerging International Standard 25964: *Structured Vocabularies for Information Retrieval* covers not only thesauri and taxonomies, but also the vocabulary components of classifications, subject headings lists and ontologies. This book by Professor Currás also addresses thesauri, taxonomies and ontologies, but from a systems-theoretic point of view, and is a welcome addition to a literature which is becoming increasingly important as we move nearer to the practicalities of the semantic web. However we may define taxonomies and ontologies, the logical structuring of concepts (for that is what the thesaurus sets out to achieve) must underpin any vocabulary used for information retrieval, be it applied to single databases or in federated searching.

This edition is therefore very timely and the author, who is knowledgeable in both information organisation and systems theory, is eminently qualified to write such a book.

Alan Gilchrist
Cura Consortium
September 2009

Preface

After a gap of a few years, I am once again devoting part of my professional activities to the subject of writing thesauri. In this day and age, in which electronic technologies rule the scene and where even the most recalcitrant users have a computer in their offices and homes with programs and applications which allow them to hold the world in their hands, it might seem totally superfluous to want to write yet again on the subject of thesauri. Experience is proving otherwise. Consider the dichotomy that exists between someone who is a user of information – i.e. data – who searches for and needs it in their daily activities, regardless of what these may be, and those who prepare this data for their respective uses. For many years, it was thought that machines could solve all those queries that arose in everyday life. This led to the idea that the knowledge or study of the subject of thesauri was, for example, something superfluous and unnecessary. Comments to the effect that 'They just want to waste time' were commonplace. If there were no experts involved in 'wasting their time', how could the machines work? As the use of mechanical and electronic gadgets became more frequent and widespread, it seemed that they had appeared out of the blue, that nobody had created them, as if it were a logical and normal thing for them to operate by themselves. I have used all these previous arguments as a means of justifying my decision to take another look, after a few years, at the subject of the theory of thesauri.

With this new work, I intend to continue along the same lines as my two previous books, *Thesauri: Terminological Languages* and *Thesauri: Handbook of Construction and Usage*, with the publication of a book aimed at teaching or serving as a guide, for experts and students alike, to what in fact are ontologies and taxonomies and their relationship with thesauri.

This new book could not be a mere copy of my previous books. My first book, published back in 1991, mirrored the uncertainties of that time, when terminology was very cordially linked with the new classification systems, based on unique and untransferable words taken from the text and which, precisely because of this, led to new terms being coined. Nowadays it is quite natural to consider a classification method, a thesaurus for instance, as a terminological language. Back then this was almost a novelty and is why my first book included some chapters on terminology. That book, as so often with my work, was considered ground-breaking in terms of its concept and interpretation. It was translated into Portuguese in Brasilia. Both the Spanish and Portuguese versions were sold out in record time. I felt that a new edition was needed, and soon.

On my visits to various documentation centres and libraries, mostly in South America, I also found photocopies of these works in beautifully bound versions. This led to the idea of writing a new book to replace those and other photocopies. However, this idea took some time to come about. The various causes for this – such as my many other teaching and professional commitments – were among the reasons why my second book on thesauri dealt solely and exclusively with their construction and usage. It was a short, dense and very practical book which came out in 1998, and which also sold out immediately.

Things have changed so much over the last few years mainly due to the influx of information technologies, and there has been such an increase in the number of experts involved in studying and organising knowledge that there is a need to reflect on these new trends and forecasts. We can no longer write exclusively about the theory of thesauri. The extensive literature available on the Internet is evidence that thesauri have to be included within a framework of concepts which were not used previously in information and document sciences such as ontologies and taxonomies.

On the subject of taxonomy, here again I was a pioneer. In my book *Information in Its New Aspects*, published in 1988, there is a chapter addressing the relationship between information technology and document sciences and taxonomy and systematics, both of them synonyms for classification systems in which thesauri play a central role. This new book begins by devoting two whole chapters to ontologies and taxonomies and how they have been influenced by electronic technologies.

Systematics cannot be left to one side, as it is a discipline in itself. Systematics has been widely studied, especially in the last 60 or 70 years, by biologists, who use it as a classification system for living creatures. To extrapolate further, it can also be applied to documents, their contents, facts … and information. A highly feasible adaptation of cladistic systematics to the structure of thesauri has been found through the study of systematics.

Let us not forget that we live in a world of interrelationships and communications, where all of human activity is subject to mutual influences. Watertight compartments have disappeared. There is no reason today to be cut off from the environment, from the world we live in, from the sphere in which we work and act. The old theory of systems has been reborn and is applied, even when we are not aware of it, to each and every human activity. For this reason, in a book whose aim is to give a true picture of our present situation, I could not overlook mentioning and applying the theory of systems – systemic science – to the theory of thesauri. Hence I have included a chapter on this subject.

Really, the novelty, relevance and importance of this book lies in its consideration of systems science and systematics in relation to ontologies, taxonomies and thesauri. This is the first book in the field of information science where these relationships are studied.

I usually treat my books as if they were my children. After all, I've given birth to them. This book comes into a world of turmoil, where ideas, some new, some old, clash and stumble over each other fighting for supremacy, and all this in a state of thoughtless confusion. I hope this book has a smooth voyage, where it can perhaps dispel this confusion and serve, above all, as a guide for reflecting on new approaches to thought and its applications.

Emilia Currás
Madrid, July 2009

Prologue

With the publication of this new book entitled *Ontologies, Taxonomies and Thesauri in Systems Science and Systematics*, Professor Emilia Currás once again brings her wide experience and knowledge of the subject to the world of information science and documentation.

The theme of thesauri is already a classic in her repertoire, and she has already written two works on the subject: *Thesauri: Terminological Languages* (1991) and *Thesauri: Handbook of Construction and Use* (1998). This present edition completes the previous viewpoints, formulating the study, principally, around two main themes: taxonomies and ontologies. Both of these are highly topical, the former because, over the past few years, we have witnessed a renewed interest in the study of taxonomies as well as the way in which they interrelate with classification systems, although these two have, in fact, always been closely linked, and the latter because it is an important, widespread knowledge information system. These were originally applied to other spheres but undoubtedly bear a close relationship to the subject addressed by the author.

The book focuses on a part of the thesaurus which is fundamental but which regrettably has rarely been broached: its conceptual structure. The structuring of this documentary language, as that of any other language, is undoubtedly one of the aspects which require most attention as it is key to enhancing the efficacy of the language later on, principally in the information retrieval process. The last two decades of the previous century saw numerous research efforts aimed at (ensuring) how the thesaurus had adapted to the new electronic information systems, where the end user faces the data retrieval process without any help from an expert. The results of these studies pointed to the need for a change in the way thesauri are constructed in order to make them more user-friendly and stressed, in particular, the need to give special emphasis to structure and the conceptual relationships expressed in that language. There is, therefore, a tendency to create highly conceptual structures. These, in turn, allow for a rich and comprehensive semantic network to be established between the terminologies which constitute its linguistic expression. If we take into account that the structure can act as an interface for data retrieval and that the semantic relationships are the routes which the user can use to browse the structure, in other words browse the system, it is patent that studies and research aimed at enhancing the structure acquire an added importance. Hence any works which share these interests and contribute to the advancement and development of these aspects are most welcome.

The first part of the book tackles the subject from a theoretical viewpoint, beginning with the study of various structures and/or structuring principles over time and goes on to focus on the ontologies and taxonomies as being, in the author's opinion, prominent structural forms.

The author leaves it to the end of her book to express an opinion which is very dear to her and which she finds especially interesting, as evidenced over the years with the publication of several studies and with her recent book *Information Science under Systemic and Systematic Hypotheses*, i.e. the General Systems Theory. It is an interesting contribution because it complements other points of view often expressed on the subject.

I would like to mention the overall tone of the work since, as the title claims, its main purpose is to enlighten students or experts in these subjects, although her potential readers undoubtedly extend far beyond the confines of these two groups. There is no question that this work will be welcomed by experts interested in these studies and by students of the various specialised branches of information science as well as by professionals interested in updating their knowledge.

Finally, I would like to thank the author for publishing this new book, born from her knowledge of and long-standing experience in the subject, and which complements other books on the topic. I would like to mention in particular the well-directed approach of the points raised and their relevance to today's demands. These pages will make for very rewarding reading by those who come upon this book.

María José López-Huertas
Universidad de Granada
Vice-President, ISKO – International

About the author

Emilia Currás holds a PhD in Chemistry and is a researcher, teacher and university professor of Information Science (LIS). She introduced LIS studies in Spain and a number of other Iberoamerican countries, is a founder of SEDIC, the Spanish Society for Information Science, and is a Fellow of the Institute for Information Scientists (UK). In addition to many Spanish accolades she is an IBI (UK) Distinguished Woman, has been decorated by the government of the Colombian Republic and has a book dedicated to her entitled *A Life: Profession and Passion*.

An Academician of the Royal Doctor's Academy, Madrid, the Royal Academy of Fine Arts and Historical Sciences, Toledo, and the Academy of Fine Arts, Brasilia, she was also Woman of Year 2004 in the USA, is Honorary President of ISKO-Spain and has received several gold and silver medals and other decorations from Asian, Middle Eastern, European and Iberoamerican LIS institutions. A Distinguished Member of the Official Chemical Spanish Association and Doctor and Teacher in the Spanish Association, she is a founder member of several Spanish LIS societies and has been invited to deliver lectures and conferences by several Asian, American, European and Middle Eastern governments.

She has held several executive positions at national and international universities and institutions. She sits on the editorial boards of several national and international publications, e.g. *Scire* (Zaragoza, Spain) and *Revista General de Sistemas* (Valencia, Spain), and is vice-president of the section for Science and Technology of ATENEO, the Cultural Spanish Society. In May 2010 she was honoured with International Peace Prize by the United Cultural Convention, USA.

As a consequence of her research she has formulated a new epistemological theory, *informationims* and a *vertical integration of science*, has also developed new educational and professional teaching methods and introduced into Spain the *general theory of systems* and *systematics* as applied to LIS.

The author may be contacted via the publishers.

From classifications to ontologies

This first chapter will deal with ways of understanding the process that started with the creation of classification methods in antiquity, and continues into modern times with the current theories and uses of ontologies within the context of information science. It is therefore important to position oneself in the centre of this theme, where knowledge organisation can be found. Consequently, the topic of knowledge itself must be taken into account: its origins, causes and the consequences it has for human cognitive activities.

When discussing classification, knowledge organisation, the formation of knowledge itself or ontologies, we must also discuss their implicit primary foundation: information. This information must be seen as the result of an intellectual and physiological activity which involves the creation of information in its generic sense due to the impact of energetic impulses on the brain which activate certain neurons. I have already explored these theories in various other books and papers (Currás, 1982, 2002, 2004).

Writing about knowledge organisation at this time of transition and transmutation to new ways of thinking is an attractive but risky undertaking. On the one hand, the concepts become broader, reaching higher levels of abstraction. On the other hand, constant invention and new discoveries trigger the emergence of new disciplines which, nevertheless, do not remain isolated in their field of knowledge, but rather integrate and interweave with one another. It is often rather difficult to establish limits and borders in this field. Specialists try to establish paradigms and metaphors on which to base their theories and opinions with the aim of moving towards new ideologies that, because they are new, have not yet been properly defined.

Knowledge

When studying a new topic, it is usually a good idea to establish a concrete base from which to develop one's reasoning. Therefore, in this case, we should start by defining the term 'knowledge organisation'. Nevertheless, it is logical to focus firstly on knowledge itself, the origin and cause of its own organisation.

Knowledge can be thought of as an intelligent mental process for the acquisition of knowledge, which is in turn an intermediate step in the formation of lines of opinion. It constitutes one of the useful quanta of information that have an impact on the mind producing knowledge and its subsequent mental processes, which cause various ways of thinking (see Figure 1.1).

However, *knowledge* also means the knowledge accumulated over time, and consequently a quasi-synonym or comparison can be established with *science* and *culture*. In my opinion, the difference between these concepts lies in the subjective nature of knowledge. It is individual and personalised, and depends in each case on the 'entity' that possesses or contains this knowledge. It is also a substratum for science and culture (see Figure 1.1).

Figure 1.1 Concept of knowledge

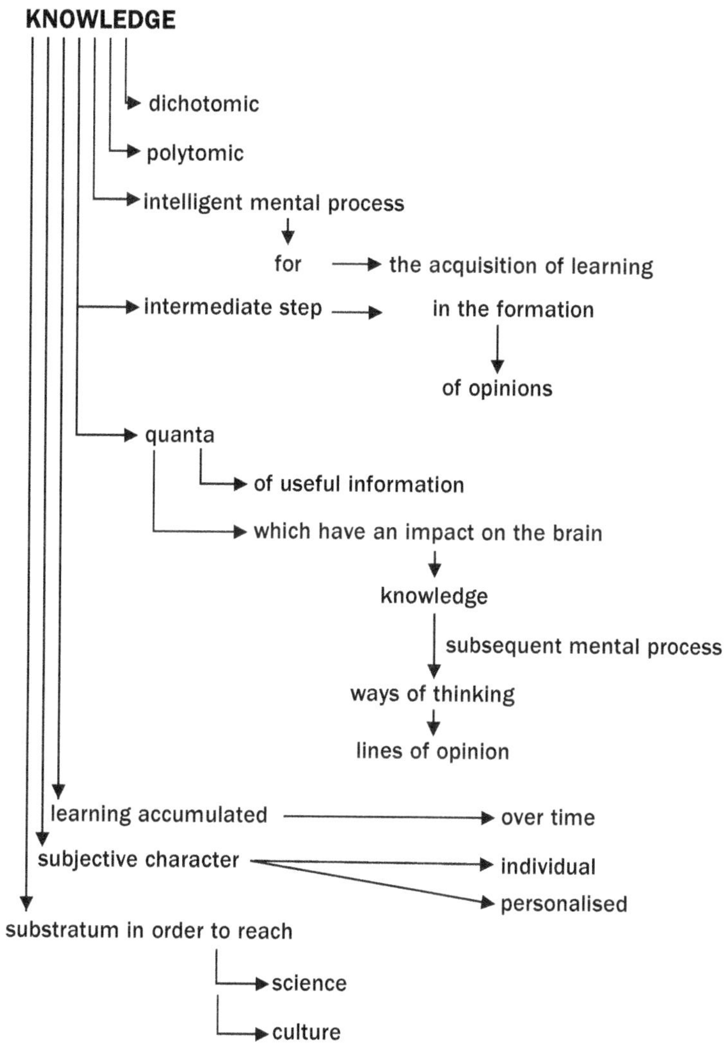

KNOWLEDGE

- dichotomic
- polytomic
- intelligent mental process
  - for ⟶ the acquisition of learning
- intermediate step ⟶ in the formation
  - of opinions
- quanta
  - of useful information
  - which have an impact on the brain
    - knowledge
      - subsequent mental process
    - ways of thinking
    - lines of opinion

learning accumulated ⟶ over time

subjective character ⟶ individual

⟶ personalised

substratum in order to reach

- science
- culture

In the creation of knowledge, western philosophers also consider the internal human condition and external agents. They believe that knowledge is obtained by means of sensations or perceptions that are received from the outside world and interpreted by each individual according to their own idiosyncrasies, adding the element 'rationality' to the process. Plato (428–348 BC), in his dialogue with Theaetetus, points out that science is converted into knowledge when reason is exerted.

During medieval times, a transition can be seen from one kind of logical thought process to another in which experience is also a feature. Albertus Magnus (1200–80), based his concept of knowledge in practical experiences, while Roger Bacon (1214–94) dealt with knowledge through lines of argument and knowledge based on experiments.

This theory continued to be prevalent during the Renaissance and subsequent periods. Kant (1724–1804), writing in the eighteenth century, comments that experience should be rationalised in order for correct knowledge to be obtained.

In subsequent centuries, this subjective quality has continued to be conferred on the concept of knowledge, and perceptions are associated with stimuli received by one or more sensory organs. Relationships are established between perception and language as a genuine form of expression and communication. Izuzquiza says that language limits our thoughts, while Coseriu suggests that language classifies reality, limiting it to our skills and attitudes. In fact, it has been proven that human beings produce more ideas than words with which to express them.

The relationship between knowledge and language is very revealing, and has importance for information science, since it establishes a concordance, a system, between those two concepts and the concept of the document, where knowledge is recorded and preserved for subsequent use in the form of language.

A new concept of knowledge

The concept of knowledge changes when computers and information technology are applied to information processes. The subjective, personal character of knowledge disappears. Indeed, the term 'knowledge base' is employed when, in reality, this is only a storage system or database for information accumulated in a computer's memory.

When Pylyshyn tells us that knowledge must be thought of as a synonym for computing, he is not wrong, given the studies on the brain's activities and functions which have been carried out for some years. Of these studies it is worth highlighting those by Pedro C. Marijuán and John Westley for their originality. These two authors focus their studies on the evolution and activity of brain cells. In summary, they suggest that a brain cell can be compared to a computer system. The RNA passed to the DNA is the 'knowledge base', which contains the stored static information. The nucleic acids make up the software and the proteins are the hardware. Within these categories, the enzymes – unstructured proteins – function as electronic circuits that also behave as rules of inference. Other protein groups work as vehicles, transmitters that convey the knowledge formed.

According to this theory, information arrives at the cell and acts as a quantum of energy, activating the cell, as in the theories posed by Szent Gyorgyi (1968), among others. Therefore, when the aforementioned process begins, new information is created, that is to say knowledge (see Figure 1.2).

Here we can see new tendencies in ways of thinking in which everything revolves around computing and cybernetics.

Figure 1.2   A new concept of knowledge

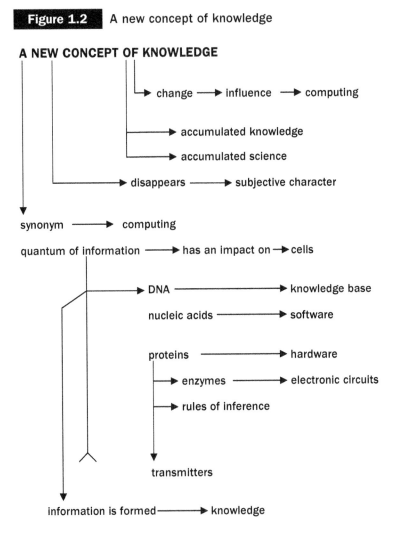

A NEW CONCEPT OF KNOWLEDGE

change → influence → computing

accumulated knowledge

accumulated science

disappears → subjective character

synonym → computing

quantum of information → has an impact on → cells

DNA → knowledge base

nucleic acids → software

proteins → hardware

enzymes → electronic circuits

rules of inference

transmitters

information is formed → knowledge

Knowledge and information

Following the thread of this way of interpreting the assimilation of information by the brain and the relationship this process has with knowledge, it is appropriate to mention some of the ideas proposed by authors in recent years which also follow this line of thought.

Of the extensive literature available on the subject, it is worth highlighting the theories of Javier García Marco (2003), who states that knowledge is information that has been integrated and personalised, ready for use: information is potential knowledge in a form which is directly proportional to its availability. This idea supposes the establishment of a circuit of knowledge and information with a linear movement, yet discontinuous in time and space, where both components form a system and information acts as an inflow and outflow vector, as well as a feedback element. This is a new and extremely interesting systemic vision. Padmini Srinivasan tells us that knowledge is included in a system of information retrieval because it allows representation and operation with the basic text objects, that is to say data (author's words). Another related point of view is that of Newell (1998). In his opinion, knowledge is the symbolic representation of information.

Ranganathan has a more theoretical and psychological perspective, as he suggests that knowledge is information deposited in the memory as a result of the association of perceptions. In various writings I too have related these two concepts, only in the opposite way. Information is the primary cause that produces knowledge when it arrives at the brain and has an impact on its neurons. Then certain processes begin to take place, either successively or perhaps simultaneously given that our concept of measurement of time adjusts itself to our mesocosmic spatial and temporal dimension, processes of perception, apprehension, analysis, classification and filing in the memory, an evaluation which consists of personal, subjective knowledge, conditioned by the individual and cultural substratum of each individual. In a subsequent, more complex mental development, knowledge becomes ideas, lines of thought. These are converted into useful information when the occasion arises.

Knowledge organisation

It is interesting to note that the concept of 'knowledge organisation' does not appear in any of the major encyclopaedias. It is necessary to refer to the terms 'science', 'learning' or 'knowledge' itself in order to find a reference to its potential 'organisation'. In contrast, in the most recent publications, numerous references to this topic can be found. It is possible that this apparent anomaly owes itself to its use in computer science and cybernetics. Likewise, it has been noted that in the vast field of librarianship and documentation, there are hardly any references to 'knowledge organisation' which are not related to the classification of documents and the topics which these documents cover. In the majority of cases, thematic 'classification system' is used as a synonym for knowledge organisation. Indeed, knowledge is confined to the thematic area of documents, and from there springs the intimate harmony between 'classification' and 'organisation'.

Nevertheless, if the different meanings of the concept of knowledge are taken into account, it is clear that there is a more profound content underlying knowledge organisation that is both philosophical and practical.

In order to formulate some ideas on contents and evolution over time with regard to knowledge organisation, it is necessary to refer back to the studies carried out on the organisation of learning, the classification of sciences or theory of knowledge, and thereby think about the different ideas and theories proposed by different thinkers from a wide variety of cultures and countries. The next step in understanding what knowledge organisation is will be to study the way in which knowledge is formed, in order to construct both a personal cognitive and a collective cultural store of knowledge.

Synthesising the ideas of various thinkers such as Wordsworth or P.S.K. Sharma, it is possible to set knowledge organisation within the mental processes that begin with perception and end with transmission. In my opinion, in each of the stages involved a biased and specific knowledge organisation is formed, which is not completely fulfilled until it is transmitted. This last phase can be argued about, since human beings do not always externalise their thoughts.

Knowledge organisation and representation

From the point of view of our western culture, the general trend in the ordering of knowledge organisation has been to divide it into two types, intelligence and sensation. Plato himself establishes this distinction in his metaphysical dualism, adding a third, practical element to the scheme: theory, practice and poetry (production). These lines, with varying numbers of variations, subdivisions and additions, have prevailed right up until modern times, although subsequent theories tend to present a knowledge organisation that is divided into pure, applied and spiritual knowledge.

The latest trend involves a unit of thought within which there are many subdivisions, branches of knowledge or disciplines, reflecting those that are emerging due to the current surge in scientific and technical developments.

The study of the presentation and representation of knowledge organisation should be observed through the prism of the presentation and representation of knowledge itself. In reality, this is an important section within the epistemology or gnoseology that has existed since ancient times, although their scope and applications have expanded.

Human beings communicate representations of their knowledge in an oral, written or graphic form which results in the use of oral, written and graphic languages. With regard to written languages, it is possible to distinguish between natural and artificial languages.

Nowadays, the range of artificial languages that have been created – and are being created on a daily basis – is growing constantly. This is a field that is rapidly emerging and evolving, mainly due to the explosion in information and the application of computer science.

- Symbolic representation of knowledge
- languages:
  - natural
  - artificial:
    - codified (e.g. computer programs)
    - classification systems (e.g. UDC, thesauri)

It is true to say that a system that classifies the thematic content of a document is a coded language. It is now worth pointing out that a computer language also serves to represent knowledge and offers a way of organising this knowledge. In this way, knowledge organisation is once again linked to computing, cybernetics and other new technologies applied to the treatment of information.

Cognitive sciences

The *organisation of knowledge*, as a primary cause and final objective of human activity, does not escape the effects of current influences. Its field of action has expanded. Firstly, modern trends tend to regard knowledge organisation from the perspective of two major fields: one being knowledge itself and the other its use. The field of knowledge retains its original philosophical and psychological roots with few modifications. The second aspect is very much affected by modern influences. For a start, today people talk about knowledge organisation within the fields of industry, business, society, science, documentation, library indexing and information technology, that is to say within the most common and essential daily tasks.

Consequently, researchers and academics have tried to deepen their knowledge of this topic, in accordance with the underlying modern concept of globalisation, and have established a new field of learning known as 'cognitive sciences'. This concept appeared around 1945 and is an algorithmisation of human thought through electronic means. The old paradigms are not appropriate for modern circumstances, and consequently a new 'cognitive paradigm' has been created, in the context of which Ingetraut Dahlberg places her 'cognitive units' and establishes 'cognitive fields' within which, in turn, 'cognitive structures' are found.

After careful consideration, it appears that the same concepts are being dealt with from a computing and information technology perspective, only using a new terminology.

Information scientists, information professionals and librarians appropriate these new ideas for themselves, and define them according to their principles and needs. For example, John P. Van Gigch associates cognitive sciences with the representation of symbols in computing. Neelemeghan says that when there is a contradiction between knowledge always thought to be true and new knowledge, which also seems to be true, a 'cognitive paradigm' should be found which will relate the two and allow their symbolic treatment. For Dahlberg, 'cognitive units' are equivalent to concepts expressed by one or more words.

'Cognitive structures' are compared to headings for the materials contained in classification systems and 'cognitive fields' to the different classes within these systems. Gopinath talks of the need for new, more accessible methods of searching for information that require new 'cognitive models' for information retrieval or, to use the classic terminology, 'search strategies'. Fugmann defines 'cognitive paradigms' in knowledge organisation as the structuring of knowledge and its components which offers flexibility in the understanding and assimilation of the demand for information. In August 1992, a conference was held in Madras, now known as Chennai, on the 'new paradigms in knowledge organisation' in which the majority of papers presented were about the structuring of very different cognitive classification systems.

In the current work, and in very general terms, it is suggested that cognitive sciences, such as interdisciplinary sciences, should be based on psychology, gnoseology, behavioural studies, computing, artificial intelligence and information science. This will be achieved using open and wide-ranging criteria encompassing new tides of opinion, controversy and criticism. Knowledge organisation should always be in harmony with society's needs at any given time, in other words knowledge organisation for knowledge organisation's sake.

Talent management

Nowadays, evolution and progress move on at high speed: this is evident in all areas, and so it seems that just when a concept, idea or way of thinking has been established and consolidated, we come across a new concept, idea or way of thinking which, at the least, attracts our attention or even wholly contrasts with previous concepts. This point must be emphasised, because recently a new concept related to talent has emerged.

The term *talent* refers to the capabilities and skills of a human being. It suggests good, specific professional training in a field of action, that is to say sound, in-depth knowledge. It is also something creative and imaginative which leads to innovation. Someone with talent has a sense of responsibility and duty. This almost perfect individual is the cornerstone of human capital and represents its economic and productive value.

It is clear that the concept of talent management has its roots in company economics. It is not so much a matter of its importance for information science as of its importance in the organisation and proper functioning of an economic or commercial entity dedicated to managing knowledge. An example of this might be a company dealing with consultancy and the informatisation of active resources in an institution in need of such services.

According to Pilar Jericó's book *La gestión del Talento* (*Talent Management*) (2000), this is a matter of finding a professional with talent and trying to get the most out of him or her, without wasting their capabilities and skills.

This question remains, in a way, out of context for our purposes in this book, as well as this chapter. Nevertheless, it is interesting to note as an illustration of the concepts that feature in our field of action.

Learning systematisation

This section refers to learning as a whole and its systematisation, taking its organisation and classification into account where these encompass knowledge and information, as well as its manual, mechanical or electronic management.

Since the beginning of time, human beings have developed mental processes that have lead to the organisation of their territory, that is to say their field of action, everything that makes up their daily lives. It is an innate quality that gives character to the human being, as an individual as well as a species. This ordering, at first unconscious, gradually became a conscious classification process through the addition of the attributes and specific characteristics of objects or thoughts. These concepts were then conceived in the mind as a reflection of the actual surroundings in which human beings live.

Eastern philosophers attribute the skill of classification to human beings as a faculty that is intrinsically human in nature. Without this skill, human beings would not be capable of distinguishing between good and bad or making choices that would help them evolve during different periods of history. Navalani and Galwani (1989) come to the conclusion that the ability to classify belongs to the divine intellect and is the first law of heaven. Richardson believes that human beings evolved and became distinct from simians because of their ability to classify things.

It is true to say that simians also possess the ability to classify, although it must be said that their minds are less developed than those of human beings.

Historical evolution

Historically, human beings have always felt the need to give expression to their knowledge in a way that would stand the test of time.

Different graphics such as cave paintings have been used precisely in order to perpetuate learning. In the context of this book, it is written expression in the form of documents that is the focus. The term 'documents containing human knowledge' will be applied to the classification of documents.

Humans have classified their world, their learning, according to their own idiosyncrasies, cultures and traditions. Our focus will be the 'known world', considered from the point of view of western civilisation (see Figure 1.3).

In the past, there was the idea of a single corpus of learning, divided up into specialities. Classifications were created according to evolution in each period of history. As a starting point, the Library of Ashurbanipal in Nineveh from around 825 BC can be cited as one of the oldest reference points. An important advance in the classification of 'volumes' is that proposed by Callimachus in the Library of Alexandria, back in the years 260–240 BC. He established a system for ordering volumes by subject matter and author. These criteria are still used today.

The idea of science, or philosophy, or learning, united to form a whole, was lost over time as the quantity of knowledge grew due to progress. A systematisation of learning, in which the difference between philosophy and science is appreciated, can be found in Raimundo Lulio's (Llull) (1235–1315 AD) *Ars Magna*. Another cornerstone can be found in August Comte's classification system (1789–1857), which is elaborate for its time, and distinguishes between the different specialities and aspects of knowledge of the period.

Within the field of library science, the Universal Classification by Dewey (1873), converted by Henri La Fontaine and Paul Otlet (1893) into the Universal Decimal Classification, is worth a mention.

From classification to knowledge organisation

It can be deduced from the study of classifications, considered regular and useful by Rosa San Segundo (1996) and other

Figure 1.3 Systematisation of learning

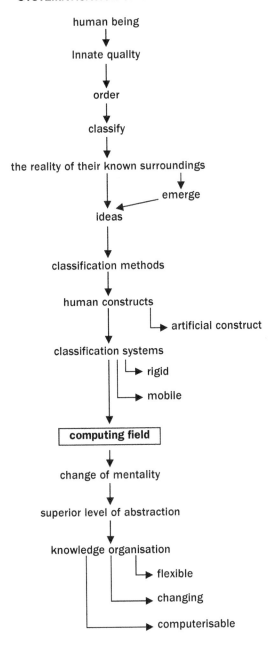

SYSTEMATISATION OF LEARNING

human being

Innate quality

order

classify

the reality of their known surroundings

emerge

ideas

classification methods

human constructs

artificial construct

classification systems

rigid

mobile

computing field

change of mentality

superior level of abstraction

knowledge organisation

flexible

changing

computerisable

authors, that they are man-made, artificial constructs that follow a rigid structure of unchanging principles.

It is true that their substructures have become more flexible in order to allow the inclusion of new concepts that are constantly arising due to progressive evolution, and everything seemed to be progressing very smoothly until electronic technology came into play with its computing, expert systems, webs, etc.

The idea of unified science and the idea of the independence of its components from each other arose simultaneously. I envisage the ordering of learning in today's world to be a federation of specialities or branches of knowledge which make up a multidisciplinary and multicultural whole, ordered vertically, related to each other and introducing codes that are ready to be electronically managed.

It is, therefore, a matter of ordering knowledge, and it does not make sense to use fundamental classifications as a foundation for this process – they have no application here. The current state of evolution requires the 'organisation of knowledge'.

This new concept of order, with its new terminology, requires a change of mentality, a rise to a higher level of abstraction to reach a more globalised and specific view of our field of action. The horizon is gradually expanded (see Figure 1.3).

Why ontologies exist

In the past few years, new terms have emerged within the field of information science, such as domains (of knowledge), engineering (of knowledge), mining (of knowledge), semantic webs, morphological fields ... and ontologies. In reality these terms are usually applied to older, well-known concepts, which give rise to the question: what would cause these changes in meaning?

The cause is the entry of information technology into the world of documentation and information. Computer scientists have begun to develop computer programs without taking into account the professionals in the fields of documentation and information. But who is really turning their backs? ... The fact is that these changes have happened, and today *ontologies* are synonyms for documentary languages, only they possess quite different structures.

It seems that with the application of computer languages to natural languages the structure of the word is broken. Now it is all about bits and groups of bytes related to each other, which acquire meaning when a coherent structure is applied to them, expressed again in the 'words' of natural language. This is an understandable process. What interests me is the application of the term *ontology* to this concept, which is also well known since ancient times in the fields of philosophy and metaphysics.

The *Diccionario Enciclopédico Abreviado de Espasa Calpe* describes ontology as that part of metaphysics that deals with the being in general and its transcendental properties. The Instituto de Ontología Aplicada (2003) says that it is the art and science of being. Its aim is to penetrate and examine the fundamental nature of being in itself. In some philosophical treaties, ontology is described as the study of what exists and what we assume exists in order to achieve a coherent description of reality.

This description may be the key to understanding the appropriation of this term by computer scientists. There is a desire to find a parallel between 'the study of what exists', that is to say a domain of knowledge, and 'what we assume exists', or the transformation from a natural language, a reality of the chosen domain, to a codified language, which is what we 'assume exists', in order to 'achieve a coherent description of reality', that is to say in order to be able to obtain a coherent 'answer' to reality (see Figure 1.4).

Perhaps this reasoning is rather contrived. However, to me it seems to be, in some way at least, an acceptable explanation, given that I have not found an alternative in the abundant literature which exists on this subject.

Figure 1.4   About ontology

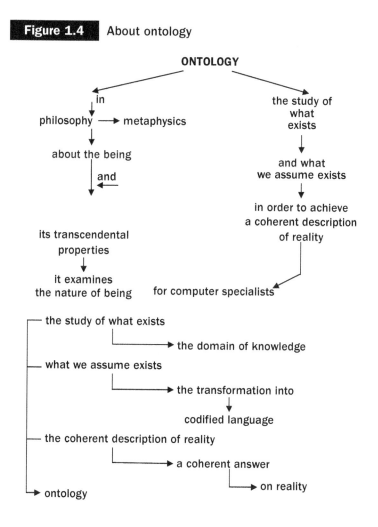

Ontologies

Modern writers on this subject do not agree on the date when ontologies were first mentioned in this new way. Vickery (1997) accepts the suggestion of 1954 as a possible date, although only as an approximation. During the 1980s, it seems that the conceptualisation of a domain as a necessary part of the acquisition of knowledge became an accepted idea. In the 1990s, and above all after 1993, in the field of expert systems, it began to be admitted that the sum of knowledge that can be found in the mind of a human expert system, when codified according to a certain method, behaves like an expert computer system. Following the conferences held since 1996, frequent references to ontologies can be found.

The *definitions* of ontologies that can be found in the literature on this subject are, however, very wide-ranging. Some of these seem more significant than others. For example:

- Sava, in 1984, presents ontology as a catalogue of any thing which serves to construct a possible world. Note the simplicity and innocence of this definition evident in the prehistory of ontologies.

- Lenat y Guha, in 1990, used ontologies to capture human knowledge based on common sense.

- Uschad thinks of ontology as a group of concepts (such as entities or attributes) and their definitions and interrelations.

- Poli (2002) is more explicit, and says that ontology is neither a catalogue of words, nor a taxonomy or a terminology, nor a list of objects. It is a general framework, a structure in which a catalogue or taxonomy can display a coherent organisation.

- In the document *http://elies.rediris.es/elies9/5-4.htm*, it is suggested that ontology is the marriage of the symbols used in natural language and the entities that they represent in the real world.

- Staab, Studer et al. (2001) state that ontologies open the way for the transition from an information point of view, focused on the organisation of knowledge, to another perspective which focuses on content, where the pieces of knowledge are interconnected, combined and united. These authors also say that it is a matter of transition from a document to pieces of content.

- Javier García Marco, in his analysis of the term ontology, says that it comes from the Greek, a compound of *logos* = description and *ontos* = everything: the science or treatment of everything.

- He thus provides us with a wide-ranging definition of ontology which is completely comprehensible: it is the systematic description of entities and their modalities, and the rules that allow the description of a specific domain in accordance with the entities and processes that allow the description of 'all' things and processes.

Alan Gilchrist tells us that ontologies have emerged from the adaptation of the work of philosophers by people involved in artificial intelligence. They have developed due to an increase in internal and external documents, the great capacity of information that is available, and the low cost of electronic mechanisms.

Lars Marius Garshol says that ontologies in computer science are models used to describe the world, and consist of bringing together themes (knowledge bases), properties and kinds of relationships.

These definitions allow an understanding of the close relationship between ontologies and classification systems, where natural language is also codified, although not using computer programs.

The structure of ontologies

If we accept that an ontology is similar to a codified and controlled documentary language, like a thesaurus for example, then it is necessary to establish a difference between the two.

This difference can be found in the structure. In thesauri, the starting point is the ordering of the terms that they contain in semantic and syntactic hierarchies and relationships. In ontologies, this ordering is done in a different way, taking certain characteristics and properties of the terms into account (see Figure 1.5).

The system MICROKOSMOS can be used as an example here, in which principal and subordinate classes are established as follows:

- Objects
  - physical order
  - mental order
  - social order
- Events
  - physical order
  - mental order
  - social order
- Properties
  - attributes (objects or events)
  - relationships (with each other)

Figure 1.5 Differences between ontologies and thesauri

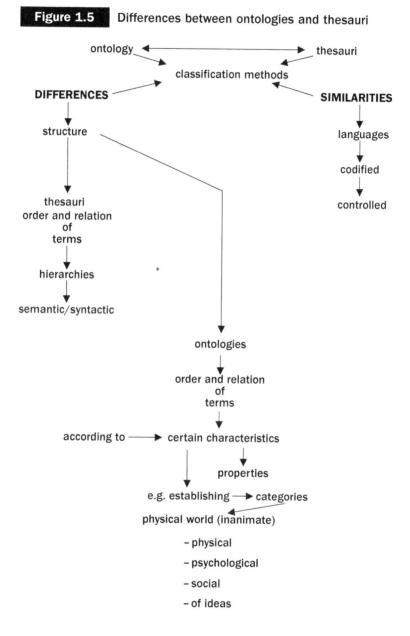

As an example, a physical object is related to a mental event, e.g. the application of a thermometer to someone with a fever.

Roberto Poli (2002) creates his structure by previously establishing some categories of concepts that should form part of an ontology organised into five ontological levels:

- physical world (inanimate)
- physical world (animate)
- psychological world
- social world
- the world of ideas.

Then the sublevels are established:

- objects
- events
- substratum
- form
- relation
- determination
- dependence
- structure
- part
- whole
- unit
- multiplicity
- dimension
- continuum
- distinct
- identity
- diversity
- possibility
- reality
- necessity
- change.

The structure of ontologies established by this author is certainly complex. Nevertheless, it serves as a good basis for understanding the differences and similarities between, for example, ontologies and thesauri.

Brian Vickery (1997) presents a different structure of ontology in which categories are ordered by levels of importance or preference:

1. Activities and processes

2. Strategies

3. Organisation

4. Market economics.

This is, therefore, an ontology that focuses on economics.

Ontologies are very useful when they are applied to translation machines, since they serve as a nexus between the words of the intervening languages in order to find similarities or equivalencies.

In the end it might be possible to establish a relationship between ontologies and thesauri, and find a similarity or dependence between them both.

Note: By way of illustration, two methods or possible ontologies that I have used in various previous works are cited. One consists of finding a code, a unifying nexus, codified language, in order to progress from chemical formulas to the computer systems of the age, by using numeric codes. This method or ontology proved to be ground-breaking in comparison with those subsequently developed. (See Currás, 1974, 1978a, 1978b.)

The other system we will use consists of creating a method or ontology in order to index 'grey literature' documents by means of a computer language, carried out in Knowledge Pro. The 63 types of grey literature included their descriptions, the institutions that produced them and models for indexing each one. This system is unique and original in its field. (See Currás, 1998b.)

Summary

Figure 1.6 summarises the evolution of the concepts and ideas presented in this first chapter.

Figure 1.6 From information to thesauri through the field of computing

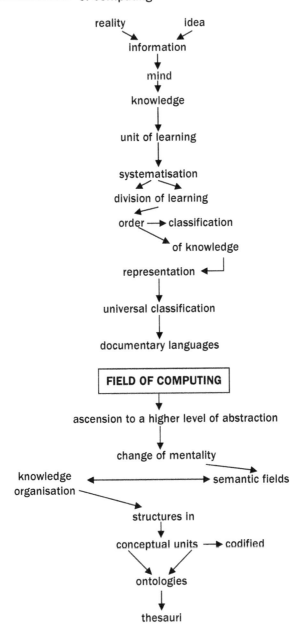

Topics for discussion

1. Give a definition of the term 'knowledge'.

2. Establish a relationship between knowledge organisation and the representation of knowledge.

3. Describe how scientific knowledge is formed.

4. Establish a relationship between useful information and knowledge.

5. Describe the difference between knowledge organisation and classification systems.

6. Establish a relationship between language and knowledge organisation.

7. Give your definition of cognitive sciences.

8. Be brave: give a definition of the concept of ontology.

9. Establish a similarity between ontology and classification systems.

10. Discuss whether you think it is correct to talk about ontologies when discussing the structure of thesauri.

11. Establish a relationship between computer languages and ontologies.

12. Describe the structure of an ontology.

References

Aguilar-López, D., López Arévalo, I. and Sosa-Sosa, V. (2009) 'Uso de las ontologías para la mejora de resultados de motores de búsqueda web', *El Profesional de la Información*, 118 (1): 34–40.

Andersen, J. (2002) 'Communication technologies and the concept of knowledge organization: a medium-theory perspective', *Knowledge Organization*, 29 (1): 29–39.

Blanco Fernández, D. (2008) 'Política y ontología. Cara y cruz de Ortega', *Revista de Filosofía*, 33 (1): 67–96.

Capurro, R. (1986) *Hermeneutik der Fachinformation*. Freiburg and Munich: Alber.

Currás, E. (1974) 'Métodos de llevar las fórmulas Químicas al Ordenador', *Afinidad*, XXXI (319): 635–42.

Currás, E. (1978a) 'Confección de un tesauro estructurado para la química', *Actas de la Conferencia Iberoamericana sobre Información y Documentación Científica y Tecnológica* (REUNIBER, 78). Madrid: CINDOC (Centro Nacional de Documentación), pp. 119–26.

Currás, E. (1978b) 'Herstellung von Einsprachigen und Mehrsprachigen Thesauri der Chemie', *Actes du Troisième Congrès Européen sur les Systèmes et Réseaux Documentaires: Franchir la Barrière Linguistique*. Luxembourg: European Commission, p. 54.

Currás, E. (1981) '¿Estaremos en la época del informacionismo?', *Revista Universidad Complutense*, 2: 186–8.

Currás, E. (1982) *Las Ciencias de la Documentación. Bibliotecología, Archivología, Documentación e Información*. Barcelona: Mitre.

Currás, E. (1985) 'Some scientific and philosophical principles of information science', *Nachrichten für Dokumentation (NFD)*, 36 (3): 151–4.

Currás, E. (1988) *La información en sus nuevos aspectos.* Madrid: Paraninfo.

Currás, E. (1995) 'Information, chaos, order', *Proceedings. Deutscher Dokumentartag 1995, Postdam.* Frankfurt am Main: Deutsche Gesellschaf für Dokumentation, pp. 545–64.

Currás, E. (1996) *Tratado sobre ciencia de la información.* Rosario: Universidad Nacional de Rosario, Argentina.

Currás, E. (1997) 'Caos y orden en la organización del conocimiento', *Organización del Conocimiento en Sistemas de Información y Documentación* (Zaragoza), ed. F.J. García Marco, 2: 13–37.

Currás, E. (1998a) 'Neurónov-Metabolizmus Informácie (Metabolismo neuronal de la Información)', *Kniznice a Informácie*, 4 (30): 145–52.

Currás, E. (1998b) 'Sistema esperto, hipermedia, para el reconocimiento, indización y recuperación de literatura gris', *Scire*, 4 (1): 117–30.

Currás, E. (2002) 'Vertical integration of sciences: an approach to a different view of knowledge organization', *Journal of Information Science*, 28 (5): 417–26.

Currás, E. (2004) 'Informacionismo y asimilación neuronal de la información', *Actas del Congreso AHDI.* Madrid: AHDI.

Díez, R.O. (1997) 'Hacia una ontología del nombre', pp. 1–9. Online at: *http://www.bu.edu/wcp/Papers/Onto/OntoDiez .htm.*

Farradane, J. (1980) 'Knowledge, information and information science', *Journal of Information Science*, 2: 75–80.

Ferreyra, D. (2003) *Las ontologías en relación con el campo de la documentación.* Misiones, Argentina: Universidad Nacional de Misiones.

Fuchs, C. (2003) 'Globalization and self-organization in the Knowledge-Based Society', *TripleC. e-journal for cognition, communication, co-operation*, 1 (2): 105–69. Online at: *http://triplec.uti.at/articles/tripleC1(2)_Fuchs.pdf*.

García Gutiérrez, A. (2002) 'Knowledge organization from a "Culture of the Border": towards a transcultural ethics of mediation'. Paper presented at the Seventh International ISKO Conference, Granada, in M.J. López-Huertas (ed.), *Challenges in Knowledge across Boundaries*. Würzburg: Ergon-Verlag, pp. 516–22.

García Marco, F.J. (2003) 'Desarrollo de ontologías orientadas a dominios específicos', in *VIII Encuentro sobre Sistemas de Información y Documentación: Modelos y Experiencias. Retos y Perspectivas*. Zaragoza: IBERSID.

Gödert, W. (2002) 'Die Welt ist gross – wir bringen Ordnung in diese Welt', *Information*, 53: 395–400.

Guerrero Bote, V. and Lozano Tello, A. (1999) 'Vínculos entre las ontologías y la biblioteconomía y documentación', IV Congreso ISKO-España. EOCONSID '99: Representación y Organización del Conocimiento en sus distintas perspectivas: su influencia en la recuperación de la información, in M.J. López-Huertas and J.C. Fernández Molina (eds), *Organización del Conocimiento en Sistemas de Información y Documentación*, 4: 25–31.

Henrichs, N. (1994) 'Informationswissenschaft als angewandte Antropologie: Der Düsseldorfer Ansetz', *Bucher für die Wissenschaft. Festschrift für Günter Gattermann*. Munich: K.G. Saur, pp. 445–61.

Henrichs, N. (2004) 'Information in der Philosophie', *Grundlagen der praktischen Information und Dokumentation*, pp. 745–9.

Instituto de Ontología Aplicada (2003) '¿Qué es la Ontología?', online at: *http://www.aplied-ontology.com/esp_whatisontology.htm*.

Jericó, P. (2000) *Gestión del talento. Del profesional con talento al talento organizado.* Madrid: Prentice Hall.

Jones, D.M., Bench-Capo, T.J.M. and Visser, P.R.S. (1998) 'Methodologies for ontology development', in J. Cuena (ed.), *Proceedings. ITi and KNOWS Conference of the 15th IFIP World Computer Congress.* London: Chapman & Hall.

Köpcke, A. (2002) 'Ontologien – inhaltliche Erschliessung in elektronischen Umgebunge', 24 Online – Tagung der Deutsche Gesellschaft für Information, in R. Schmidt (ed.), *Content in Context: Perspektiven der Informationsdienstleistung.* Frankfurt am Main: Deutsche Gesellschaft für Information, pp. 323–39.

La Ontología (2000), 5 (4): 1–13, online at: *http://elies.rediris.es/elies9/5-4.htm.*

López Alonso, M.A. (2003) 'Integración de herramientas conceptuales de recuperación en la web semántica: tesauros conceptuales, ontologías, metadatos y mapas conceptuales', in *VIII Encuentro sobre Sistemas de Información y Documentación: Modelos y Experiencias. Retos y Perspectivas.* Zaragoza, IBERSID.

Lozano Tello, A. (2003) 'Ontologías en la Web Semántica', *Jornadas de Inteligencia Web '01*, May, pp. 283–7, online at: *http://www.informandote.com/jornadasIngWEB/artículos/jiw02.pdf.*

Maedche, A. and Staab, S. (2000) 'Mining ontologies from text', in R. Dieng and O. Corby (eds), *Knowledge Acquisition, Modeling and Management. Proceedings of the 12th International Conference*, Juan-Les-Pins, France, pp. 189–202. (Lecture notes in *Computer Science 1937.*)

Martín, R., Martínez, B. et al. (2003) 'El desarrollo de una ontología a base de un conocimiento enciclopédico parcialmente estructurado', *Jornadas de tratamiento y*

recuperación de la información, online at: *http://dois.minas
.ac.uk/DoIS/data/Papers/doijotrisy:2003:p65-72.html.*

Morán, O. and Hassan, H.A. (1999) 'De una ontología
empírica a una ontología objetiva', pp. 1–36, online at:
*http://www.geocities.com/Athens/Delphi/6082/ontologia
.html.*

Moreno Ortiz, A. (2008) 'Ontologías para la terminología:
por qué, cuándo, cómo', *Revista Tradumatica*, 6.

Navalani, R. and Gidwani, N.N. (1989), online at:
http://www.library.yale.edu/humanities/sariabid.html.

Neelameghan, A. and Prasad, K.N. (eds) (2001) *Content
Organization in the NEW Millenium.* Bangalore: Sarada
Ranganathan Endowment for Library Science.

Newell, A. (1998) 'The knowledge level', *Artificial
Intelligence*, 18: 87–127.

'Ontología informática', *Enciclopedia Libre Universal en
Español* (2008), online at: *http://enciclopedia.us.es.*

Pedraza Jiménez, R., Codina, L.L. and Rovira, C. (2007)
'Web semántica y ontologías en el proceso de la
información documental', *El Profesional de la
Información*, 16 (6): 569–78.

Pérez Gutiérrez, M. (2002) 'La Información como fundamento
cognitivo de una definición adecuada al conocimiento',
paper presented at the Seventh International ISKO
Conference, in M.J. López-Huertas (ed.), *Challenges in
Knowledge Representation and Organization for the 21st
Century: Integration of Knowledge across Boundaries.*
Würzburg: Ergon-Verlag, pp. 49–57.

Polí, R. (2002) 'Ontological methodology', online at:
http://www.informatik.uni-ter.de.html.

Qin, J. (2002) 'Evolving paradigms of knowledge
representation and organization: a comparative study of
classification, XML/DTD, and ontology', paper

presented at the Seventh International ISKO Conference, Granada, in M.J. López-Huertas (ed.), *Challenges in Knowledge Representation and Organization for the 21st Century: Integration of Knowledge across Boundaries.* Würzburg: Ergon-Verlag, pp. 465–71.

San Segundo Manuel, R. (1996) *Constitución de la realidad en la era tecnológica de la posinformación.* Madrid: Ed. Universidad Carlos III.

Sánchez Cuadrado, S., Morato Larga, J., Palacios Madrid, V., Llorens Morillo, J. and Moreira González, J.A. (2007) 'De repente, ¿todos hablamos de ontologías?', *El Profesional de la Información*, 16 (6): 561–8.

Sánchez Jiménez, R. and Gil Urdician, B. (2007) 'Lenguajes documentales y ontologías', *El Profesional de la Información*, 16 (6): 541–50.

Shapiro, J.J. (2002) 'Interdiciplinary knowledge integration and intellectual creativity', paper presented at the Seventh International ISKO Conference, Granada, in M.J. López-Huertas (ed.), *Challenges in Knowledge Representation and Organization for the 21st Century: Integration of Knowledge across Boundaries.* Würzburg: Ergon-Verlag, pp. 100–6.

Srinivasan, P. (1992) 'Knowledge organization for information retrieval', *Cognitive Paradigms in Knowledge Organisation.* Madras: Sarada R.E. for Library Science, pp. 81–94.

Staab, S., Studer, R. et al. (2001) 'Knowledge processes and ontologies. Knowledge management', *IEEE Intelligent Systems*, January–February, pp. 26–34.

Svenonius, E. (2000) *The Intellectual Foundation of Information Organization.* Cambridge, MA: MIT Press.

Szent Gyorgyi, A. (1968) *Bioelectronic.* New York: Academic Press.

Tramullas, J. (1999) 'Agentes y ontologías para el tratamiento de la información: clasificación y recuperación en Internet', contact: *webmaster@jabato.unizar.es*.

Vickery, B.C. (1997) 'Ontologies', *Journal of Information Science*, 23 (4): 277–86.

Wilson, T.D. (2003) 'Philosophical foundations and research relevance: issues for information research. *Journal of Information Science*, 29 (6): 445–2.

2

Taxonomies and thesauri

Taxonomy is another concept which has experienced a change in meaning with the onset of the computer age. In this case, the term has experienced an increase in its field of action. The use of taxonomy in its classic form as applied – almost exclusively – to biology and logic has evolved to include its application to electronic technology. Thus the term taxonomy has begun to be used in the context of Information Science, specifically with regard to classification systems (see Figure 2.1).

The application of the term taxonomy to systems used for the classification of subjects is a topic which until now has been discussed by very few specialists in information and documentation. One example of its treatment can be found in my book *Documentación y metodología de la investigación científica* (*Documentation and Methodology of Scientific Investigation*), written in 1985, where I refer to the relationship between taxonomy and classification systems. However, the term has been increasingly used over the last few years, above all in conjunction with the concepts of information architecture and mining of information, and always in the context of knowledge organisation in companies and institutions. Above all, the term has been used in the context of semantic webs.

Recently, professionals in Information Science have in fact taken their concept of taxonomy from computer scientists who have found in taxonomy a solution to their classification

Figure 2.1   Concept of taxonomy

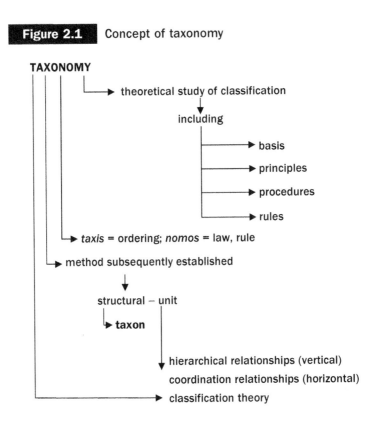

problems, especially when it comes to the ordering of conceptual units. They extract conceptual units from documents in order to facilitate the construction of computer programs for the indexing and retrieval of information.

From ordering to taxonomy

Taxonomy is, therefore, a very relevant issue in modern times, and it is necessary to examine the concept in its main traditional context in order to understand its subsequent application within the general context of Information Science.

Following a logical process, working from the lowest to highest complexity, means dealing first with ordering, then classification and classification systems, eventually reaching taxonomy. Classification systems include general or universal systems and specific systems based on isolated conceptual units, terms or their components, structured according to certain methods.

Therefore *ordering* requires a physical process which consists of assigning each entity – whether real or abstract – to a location. If we are dealing with a real entity – such as a book – its ordering means finding it a place on a bookshelf. If we are dealing with an abstract entity – such as a thought, for example – then it will be organised in order to occupy a place in our mind or in written form if we want it to endure. *Classification* represents a higher level of complexity because it can be defined as an ordering process carried out through the application of a particular method. This method implies a process of comparison of the elements to be classified in order to determine similarities and differences between them, which will in turn determine the position of certain elements in relation to others.

Note: It is convenient to adopt this definition of classification in this case, which is similar to the definition proposed in Chapter 1, but a little more appropriate to our current purposes.

The method to be used, the *classification system*, is decided on beforehand as a pre-coordinated system that can be used for any kind of entity, whether real or abstract.

The origins of taxonomy

Taxonomy, etymologically speaking, comes from the Greek *taxis* = ordering and *nomos* = law, norm, rule. In the available literature on the subject we can also find the terms 'taxinomy' and 'taxenomy', which without a doubt have their roots in the different endings that the original Greek expression would have gained from the different cases of its declension. Alvarado Ballester (1967) defines taxonomy as 'the theoretical study of a system, including its basis, principles, procedures, and rules'. It is also defined as *classification theory* (see Figure 2.2).

Thus, once again, the topic moves to a higher level of abstraction. It is no longer sufficient to establish a method of classifying entities (in biology these would be living things or their structures): it is also necessary to carry out a theoretical study which takes any other relevant aspects into

Figure 2.2 Taxonomy in information and documentation science

INFORMATION AND DOCUMENTATION SCIENCE

taxonomy

taxon

conceptual unit

data
document

different from

a unit of information

must be transmitted

vertical structure

Dewey's classification

Universal Decimal Classification

horizontal structure

classification by facets

classification by single term

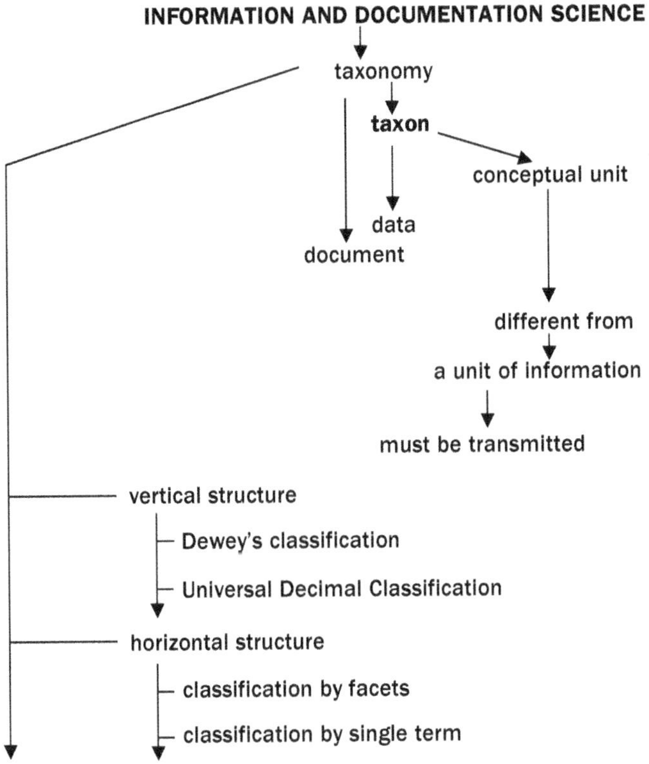

account. The term taxonomy was coined by A. De Candolle in 1813 in order to design the rules or laws to be used in systematics. Since then it has been used almost exclusively as a component of biology. Nevertheless, within the field of logic it has a wider meaning.

Using taxonomy it is possible to develop methods established after the fact, once the classificatory elements are known. The determinants of order are not decided beforehand. It is important to take the individuality and specific characteristics of the entities to be ordered into account. A structural unit is decided on, which will also represent the classification unit which Crowson (1970), among others, defines as a *taxon*.

Using taxonomy it is possible to establish categories within a classification depending on how relationships of similarities (the interaction principle), or relationships of interdependence (the duality principle), will be determined. In the first case, a classification would be achieved in a horizontal direction representing the correlation between the taxa. In the second case, a hierarchy will be used which establishes a scale from greatest to smallest, from superior to inferior entity, which will give a sense of collectivity and generality, in contrast to the previous case where a sense of individuality is achieved.

Hierarchical and horizontal order

In a taxonomy with a hierarchical order, the taxon to be used should be decided on first of all, along with the desired level of subdivision. In the field of chemistry, for example, it would be necessary to determine whether the taxon will be an element, a molecule, an atom, etc., and whether subdivisions above or below are going to be created, in order to subsequently establish the rules and laws of classification. In Information Science the taxon could be:

- a taxon in a conceptual unit

which would be the most logical choice, although it could also be:

- taxon = data or document.

The term conceptual unit (concept unit, expressed by the terms, or parts of terms, of any given language) should not be confused with the idea of a unit of information. A unit of information can be simple or complex and consist of one or more conceptual units. On the other hand, there is no information if it is not perceptible. That is to say, a conceptual unit can exist on its own, but a unit of information cannot: it must be recorded in a receiving subject and, consequently, transmitted by an emitting agent (see Figure 2.2).

In the context of this study, taxonomical methods with a horizontal structure dealing with the correlation between taxa would refer to classifications, facets and keywords. In contrast, great classifications such as that of Dewey, the Universal Decimal Classification and the classification used by UNESCO have a hierarchical, vertical, taxonomic structure.

Correlation with classifications

It is now worth specifying some concepts and details in order to better establish the correlation between taxonomy and classifications.

Durand de Gros (1899) is one of the scientists who have established the basis for taxonomy including:

- *order of generality* – where the taxa are natural elements which are ordered from greatest to smallest;

- *order of composition* – where only concrete objects are used to form the taxa.

A relationship between the whole and the part – and vice versa – is established:

- *order of genealogy*;
- *order of evolution* – where the taxa are treated according to their origin.

These form the basis for relationships of:

- hierarchy or subordination;
- coordination; and
- polarity.

Taxonomy allows us to consider:

- a system – creating an artificial order (belonging to the group ordered); or
- a method – taking a natural order into account (for ordering real things or objects).

On the other hand, taxonomic groups consist of entities characterised by a certain reality, due to the fact that the taxa used as a starting point have real characteristics. The relationship between these real characteristics is arbitrary and depends on the criteria decided on by some person, meaning that they are highly subjective. It must also be taken into consideration that taxonomic criteria are modified over time, which gives them a great adaptability and flexibility. Taxa also possess a series of fixed characteristics that are related to each other by means of successive and parallel, synthetic (or scientific) and analytical (or easily observed) operations.

Once the taxon has been defined within information sciences as a:

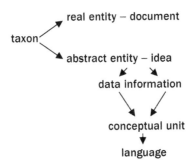

relationships based on similarities can be established which can be used to demonstrate that taxonomy fits in perfectly within these sciences, forming an integral part of them. However, it would seem that when we classify the contents of a document by means of keywords we are not creating a taxonomy, and that both concepts are at odds with each other. This would not be true. We must therefore vary a part of our previous reasoning in order to be able to apply taxonomic principles to this case.

This variation would involve proposing that the keywords, or terms, are synthetic (or scientific) taxa that can be applied to the contents of a document as a whole. On the other hand, these keywords are structured as families that demonstrate an interdependence with each other, which means that they are not isolated and variable taxa, but fixed and structural, characterised by pre-established relationships.

The document will form part of a taxon with analytical, real and observable characteristics.

In this way, everything becomes much clearer, and it can be said that taxonomy is a formal part of Information Science mainly within the context of classification methods, and therefore within thesauri.

Taxonomy in computer science

Looking back over history, it seems that in the late 1950s and early 1960s references to taxonomical classification techniques could already be found within the field of computing. This data cannot be entirely confirmed by research carried out on the Internet. Nevertheless, from 1970 onwards, and above all since the 1980s, references to the application of taxonomy in the development of computer programs are abundant.

When searching on the Internet using the terms taxonomy and computing, numerous references appear within the most varied fields of knowledge, including traditional sciences such as natural science. If the term 'information science' is added, the results are considerably limited. This has a simple explanation. We are still only beginning to realise what taxonomy means, and the importance that it can have in the organisation of indexing and information search systems using, for example, semantic webs (see Figure 2.3).

Computing taxonomy

It is certain that the first people to use the help of taxonomy in order to organise their documents were those working in the administration departments of companies. They found, perhaps, that they had a series of documents of all different kinds – contracts, bills, technical reports, etc. – that had to be organised in a coherent way in order to be located at a later date.

Computer scientists were the ones who gave them a hand with taxonomy, studying their structure and characteristics with the aim of applying them to those information needs. A whole theory of taxonomy has been developed with its own

Figure 2.3 Taxonomy in computing

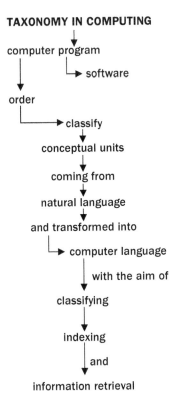

definitions and structures. In the literature on this subject definitions can be found that aid an understanding of the orientation that it is hoped can be achieved.

A *taxon* is defined as 'one or more organisms – in a broad sense of the word – that belong to the same taxonomical unit'. Likewise, it can be defined as a simple or compound unit within a field of knowledge.

In relation to our context, it is appropriate to define a taxon as a conceptual unit with semantic characteristics that belongs to any given speciality. This conceptual unit could be expressed as:

- a lexical root;
- a word; or
- a compound of the two.

Definitions

Among the common definitions of taxonomy that can be found on the Internet is the classic definition which we may use as a starting point for new reasoning.

- Taxonomy is a scientific field which classifies life (taken to mean all human ideas and activities).

- Likewise, it is defined as a controlled language, an organised list of words and phrases, or notation systems, that is used as the basis for an indexing and information retrieval process. It is organised into controlled levels.

- It can also be a navigation scheme ordered into a hierarchy (a very limited definition).

- Another significant definition says that taxonomies are conceptual structures adapted for use in semantic webs.

- Equally, taxonomy can be defined as the thing that organises documents into a thematic order, creating taxonomic levels that help with their treatment in computing.

- A utilitarian definition considers taxonomy to be a cooperative and reusable tool, independent of the domain or field in which it is applied.

- Finally, we could also consider taxonomies to be the creator of order in the chaos that is represented by conceptual units pertaining to very varied documents.

In Tema Tres (2004) there is a definition that is appropriate to the aims of this book. It describes a taxonomy as a web application for the management of documentary languages, focused specifically on the development of hierarchical thesauri. It can also be used for the development of structures for web navigation or as a complementary coordination tool in a contents manager.

It is also important to mention the definition of corporate taxonomy as the main theme in information architecture within businesses. Its mainstays are the management of knowledge, its organisation and particular characteristics.

In all these definitions the concept of *semantic webs* is implicit or explicit, giving meaning to the Internet, and making it possible for all web agents to understand the information contained therein. On the other hand, by means of webs it is possible to harmonise the semantic contents of websites, navigate them and extract information from them, adapting automatically to any potential changes in these websites (see Figure 2.4).

Note: The references consulted include the documents found on the Internet on different websites related to these topics. Other definitions are the result of this author's thoughts on the subject.

Virtual taxonomy, cybernetic taxonomy

A *virtual taxonomy* could be described as an intelligent agent or an intelligent meta-search engine to be used for web pages. It is also a form of representing knowledge by organising, analysing and structuring descriptors.

Figure 2.4 Computing taxonomy

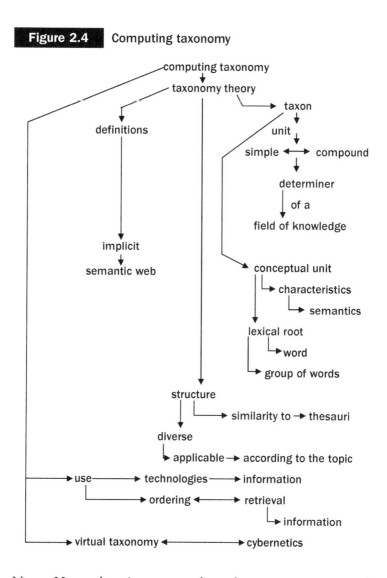

Note: Here, descriptors can be taken as a synonym for conceptual units. However, they can only be synonyms in a very few cases. A descriptor has less conceptual content than a domain.

The adjective 'virtual' actually supposes a normal utilisation of computer technology. Here, the union of both concepts – that is to say, taxonomy and computing – is once again emphasised.

With regard to *cybernetic taxonomy*, on the Internet a chance discovery led me to a document written by Ginouves and Martin (1992) on taxonomy applied to an education system, which is interesting as it gives an idea of how to describe structures in cybernetic taxonomy and is applicable to any other taxonomy in any domain. Its justification requires the systematisation of a certain structure which would contain the different levels of intellectual complexity that any given topic represents. The following divisions are established: functional taxonomy according to levels of specificity: cognitive domain, emotional domain, psychomotor domain. All this implies a challenge in field studies. There is an underlying and progressive complexity that considers both a cross-cutting, horizontal aspect and an incremental, vertical aspect.

Note: There is perhaps a similarity with the known classification structures such as thesauri. Nevertheless, the principal classes differ considerably.

Another example of the structure of a taxonomy, in this case also applied to education, can be found in the taxonomy of 'educational webs', where the following classes are established: dimensions – descriptive, pedagogical, cognitive and communicative.

Taxonomy in Information Science

In Information Science, references to taxonomies are beginning to be found, almost always in the context of the representation and organisation of knowledge in economic spheres.

Some information researchers have been carrying out research into the application of computer taxonomy to the topics they are studying. In order not to forget this fact, and as a matter of respect, I would like to mention Temprano and Badillo (1986) as pioneers in these research topics.

It is worth mentioning some of the examples found which demonstrate the wide variety of classes employed.

Of these examples, the one that is most relevant to our purpose is entitled 'Information Science Taxonomy', wherein the following divisions or categories are established: information science research, knowledge organisation, the information profession, societal uses, the information industry, information technologies, electronic information systems and services, subject-specific sources and applications, libraries and library services, etc. From here on, by means of successive subdivisions that structure the whole topic, it becomes a scientific discipline.

Another taxonomy developed in Germany, mainly for use in libraries, is the 'Beatz Biblionetz: Towards a Taxonomy for Computer Science', wherein conceptual units are ordered as follows: topics, people, books, texts and concepts (keywords). It is a method that is totally orientated towards the use of machines. It aims to establish the relationship between man and machine.

The following example, which is crucial to an understanding of how taxonomy is applied to our field of action, is 'The DELTA System: A Computer Generated Description'. DELTA stands for 'Description Language for Taxonomy'.

I will now quote briefly from this work which will prove useful in aiding an understanding of this topic, and serve to formulate subsequent reasoning:

Taxonomy: (is) a system constructed out of keywords, which in turn are structured, that is to say they form a thesaurus, in order to locate information in a particular structured network (DELTA) within a Web system. Its aims include the generation and reproduction in written form of descriptions and 'rules' to be used in the classification of programmes and the construction of packets that can be used for the interactive identification and retrieval of information. It was developed by SCIRO/the Division of Entomology between 1971 and 2000. The combination and insertion of new headings is controlled. Phrases and paragraphs are used instead of isolated terms. It can be organized in order to be used for a particular speciality or field of work.

From all the examples that have been mentioned so far some valuable lessons can be learned, perhaps leading to new research projects. The field is wide open.

Similarities between taxonomies and thesauri

Within the context of this work, it is fundamental to compare both topics and establish positive or contradictory correlations between them which will help to discern the reason for their use within the scope of our disciplines and specialised sciences.

With regard to the *similarities* between taxonomies and thesauri, the most obvious is that both have a common usage, that is they serve as a method of classifying language. Language is contained in documents which in turn contain data, potential information, which in turn has the potential to become useful information.

Some other similarities are listed below:

- Both topics are used for the systematisation of knowledge using scientific, logical and coherent methods, established by means of predetermined rules.
- Both are also pre- and post-coordinated systems made up of terms from documentary languages.
- Equally, both have a fundamental use in the evolution of the human being, promoting the development of science, investigation and innovation.

This reasoning is by no means far-fetched, since in order to carry out the above developments, an information search is necessary. If the documents – regardless of their type – are not correctly indexed it becomes impossible to carry out an effective search for information.

Consequently, both are examples of indexing and retrieval systems used for both documents and useful information.

Differences between taxonomies and thesauri

If there are so many similarities between the two, what are the *differences* between them?

The first and primary difference is that information technology is almost exclusively used in the development of taxonomies. Thesauri can be constructed manually or mechanically. Of course, more and more computer programs are emerging each day for the automatic construction of thesauri. But we must not fool ourselves: to be able to create one of these programs it is necessary to have an in-depth knowledge of the mechanism, the techniques, the theory and the practice that accompany the construction of thesauri (see Figure 2.5).

Figure 2.5 Differences and similarities between taxonomies and thesauri

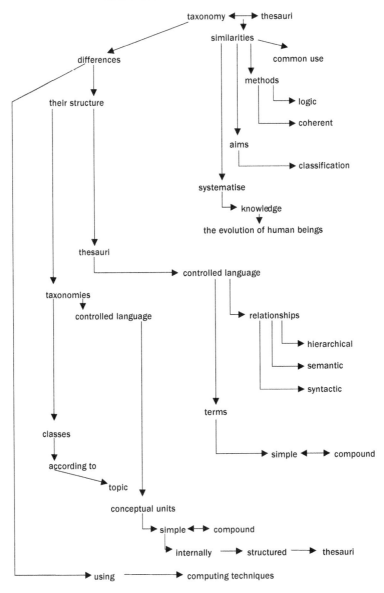

Even today we can see a difference between these two methods of ordering in relation to their use. Taxonomies are almost exclusively used by computer specialists within businesses, while thesauri are the patrimony of specialists in information and documentation, including librarians.

Nevertheless, when existing taxonomies are studied, and despite the fact that they are seen as being different to classification structures, they do involve a kind of ordering of conceptual units, similar to that of keywords, according to a hierarchy and accompanied by parallel connections of semantic and syntactic relationships. That is to say, they implicitly contain a thesaurus within them (see Figure 2.5).

Note: In order to better understand what a thesaurus, a taxonomy and an ontology are, it is advisable to consult the article 'Thesauri, taxonomies, and ontologies: an etymological note', by Alan Gilchrist (2003).

Topics for discussion

1. Establish a difference between a taxonomy and a thesaurus.

2. What is the difference between a virtual and a cybernetic taxonomy?

3. Give a definition of a taxonomy.

4. How many classes of taxon do you know?

5. Establish a difference between a classification system and a taxonomy.

6. Establish a relationship between taxonomy and computer science.

7. Make a distinction between a conceptual unit and a term.

8. Do you think that a taxonomy can be an item of software?

9. Give the outline of a possible structure for a taxonomy applied to the economy.

10. Establish a similarity between a taxonomy and a thesaurus.

11. What could be the reason for using taxonomies in information science?

12. Do you think that a taxonomy implicitly contains a thesaurus?

References

Aldana, J.F., Roldán, M.M. et al. (2002) 'Metadata functionality for semantic web integration', paper presented at the Seventh International ISKO Conference, Granada, in M.J. López-Huertas (ed.), *Challenges in Knowledge Representation and Organization for the 21st Century: Integration of Knowledge across Boundaries.* Würzburg: Ergon-Verlag. pp. 298–304.

Alvarado Ballester, R. (1967) *Sistemática, taxonomía, classificación y nomenclatura*, lecture. Madrid: Ed. Universidad de Madrid, Facultad de Ciencias.

Badillo, M. and Temprano, E. (1986) Online at: *http://www .infodoc.es*.

Batley, S. (2003) 'Taxonomies as a means of facilitating organisational information and knowledge sharing', *VIII Encuentro sobre Sistemas de Información y Documentación: Modelos y Experiencias. Retos y Perspectivas.* Zaragoza: IBERSID.

Building and Developing a Corporate Taxonomy (2004) Online at: *http://www.Aslib.com*; contact: *nadamides@ aslib.com*.

Crowson, A.R. (1999) *Classification and Biology.* London: Heinemann Educational.

Currás, E. (1985) *Taxonomía. Documentación y metodología de la investigación científica*, cuaderno de trabajo. Madrid: Paraninfo.

Currás, E. (2001) 'Integración vertical de las Ciencias. Una aproximación científica (desde una visión sistémica)', *Anales de la Real Academia de Doctores*, 5: 233–50.

Durand de Gros, J.P. (1992) *Aperçus de taxonomie général* (texte imprimé). Paris: F. Alcan.

Fink, O. (2002) 'Evaluieren–Strukturieren–Kategorisieren: Terminologie–Informationslogistik und automatische Textzusammenfassung', 24 Online Tagung (Congress) der Deutsche Gesellschaft für Information un Dokumentation, in R. Schmidt (ed.), *Content in Context. Perspektiven der Informationsdienstleistung*. Frankfurt am Main: Deutsche Gesellschaft für Information und Dokumentation, pp. 185–93.

Garshol, L.M. (2004) 'Metadata? Thesauri? Taxonomies? Topic maps! Making sense of it all', *Journal of Information Science*, 30 (4): 378–91.

Gilchrist, A. (2003) 'Tesauri, taxonomies and ontologies', *Journal of Documentation*, 56 (1): 7–18.

Gilchrist, A. (2003) 'Taxonomies and information architecture', *Scire*, 9 (1): 37–40.

Ginouves, R. and Martin, R. (1992) *Dictionnaire methodologique d'Architecture grecque et romaine*. Athens: Ecole française d'Athenes.

López Alonso, M.A. and Mares Martín, J. (1998) 'La organización del conocimiento contenido en la información hipertextual de Internet', *Jornadas Españolas de Documentación*. Online at: *http://fesabid98.florida-uni.es/Comunicaciones/ma_lopez.htm*.

Tema Tres (2004) 'Aplicación libre para la gestión de lenguajes documentales'. Online at: *http://www.r020.com.ar/tematres/index.php.2004*; contact: *info@ro20.com.ar*.

Tracey, E. (2001) 'Taxonomies for business', *Multimedia Information and Technology*; see also *Knowledge Organization*, 28 (2): 107.

Wilson, T. (2002) 'Information science and research methods', online at: *http://informationr.net/tdw/publ/papers/slovak02.html*.

3

Thesauri

In the foregoing chapters it has become evident that there is a close relationship between ontologies, taxonomies and thesauri. In fact, although there are differences between these three classification systems, all three enclose a structure made up of conceptual units, as in the case of thesauri. Their conceptual units are converted into terms insofar as they are expressed by specific words for each subject or theme. These terms are related to each other in one way or another, and in this way they resemble the relationships established in thesauri. It is therefore necessary to know what a thesaurus is, and how it is constructed and used.

Moreover, the use of computer languages devised for the construction of Internet databases and extranet systems means that it is necessary to know which conceptual units in the domain or field of reference are going to be used and how these relate to each other in order to obtain an ideal indexing system. This index will later favour an efficient information search. All of this can be achieved if we know how a thesaurus is constructed and managed. An example of the usefulness of thesauri is provided by the company Yahoo, which processes software for Internet searches, which implies an information architecture constructed on three base concepts: ontology, taxonomy and thesauri.

This reasoning serves to highlight the usefulness, even the necessity, of studying the theory of thesauri, of knowing what they are and how they are constructed and used. Information professionals, librarians, archivists and even users should also be acquainted with these matters.

Therefore we will now go on to discuss thesauri.

Terminology in classification systems

The relationship between terminology and thesauri is also close, since in reality a thesaurus is a material classification system made up of terms connected in a certain way. It also, therefore, involves a terminological language.

In fact, the expression 'terminological language' has been applied to material classification systems for some time. This usage is correct in that a terminological language is a linguistic system in which the main components are terms. We also know that these systems can be defined, according to Dahlberg, as 'primary elements of knowledge for the storage of learning' or, according to Felber, as 'linguistic units of a specialised vocabulary'.

Nevertheless, it may be interesting to stop for a moment to consider how we have arrived at this point in the evolution of terminology and classification systems. In my opinion, we are once again faced with the consequences of the evolutionary processes of our times and the accelerated rhythm of scientific, technical and humanistic events. It is once again necessary to refer to the already famous 'information explosion'.

Not so long ago, in the period between the two world wars of the twentieth century, it was the documents that contained information that had the greatest importance. Their classification, that is to say their allocation into classes according to their contents, was one of the main tasks of professionals who worked with these documents. It was at this time that people began to believe that the document was just a vehicle, a medium for its thematic content which was converted into useful and necessary information because of its own meaning and demand for its subsequent use. In the same way, the idea began to spread that it was not books that were important, but their content. Content should be dissociated from its container and considered as a separate theme. It was necessary to break down the bibliography into pieces and order it systematically.

This change in mentality and ways of thinking accelerated after the end of the Second World War, mainly due to the huge technological advances that occurred at that time. In truth, the existing thematic classifications were too rigid, too static, to include these new inventions and discoveries, the new concepts and new terms that were emerging on a daily basis. So the idea developed of taking the content out of a document and representing it in words – keywords or terms – that would subsequently be submitted to an ordering process. This process accelerated when information technology began to come into use, mainly in the form of computers.

All the words – terms – that referred to a theme and formed a part of a specialised vocabulary in turn made up a specialised language. It could soon be observed that these languages should be structured in some way, relating the terms in a logical manner so that they could be easily located within the language itself and during its subsequent use. From the natural language used in documents, we moved on to the structured language of the information contained within them.

Terminological languages

Thus expressions such as 'controlled language', 'normalised language' and 'information language' emerged, which were mainly applied to these classification systems. The conventional classification systems such as Universal Decimal Classification demanded a place in this informational/ terminological world. Eventually, these methods were also used to classify the material contained in documents.

The abundant reading available on these concepts does not contribute any enlightening ideas to these issues. In general, it seems that these texts are aimed at experts with a certain knowledge of the topics involved, and that they only intend to highlight one point or another in order to focus on particular aspects.

However, it is not only experts who are interested in classification systems or information languages. I am thinking in particular of the schoolchildren, university students and other professionals of the future who might be interested in information sciences for their own ends. Today, personal computers represent a great tool for the ordering of books or documents, even within the home. For these reasons it is worth trying to systematise this theme, and deal with it starting from its most fundamental principles.

We will start by establishing some definitions that will be useful in subsequent reasoning.

It could be said that *controlled language* means:

- a language in which the elements – words – that it is made up of are controlled in accordance with some pre-established rules.

It could also be defined as:

- a linguistic system in which the units that it is composed of are structured according to some pre-established rules.

As long as the same 'rules' are always used, rules that are predetermined according to logical and coherent criteria, we should refer to a normalised language. The units that it is composed of become terms. Consequently *normalised language* is:

- a controlled language to which logically predetermined rules are applied and whose linguistic units are terms;
- a linguistic system made up of terms that are related to each other according to logically pre-established rules.

Thus we can see that these systems have their reason for being in their use for classification in the field of documentation. From this we can deduce that *information language* is:

- a controlled – normalised – language used for classification in the broadest sense of the word.

If we go one step further, we find ourselves dealing with information operations, which include indexing and information retrieval. In the end, all these ideas were the results of the concerns and interest raised by the search for information and the documents required for the development of any given activity.

These would have to be correctly indexed and classified. This gave rise to:

- *indexing languages*;
- *information retrieval languages*.

Being languages, these do not require any further definition.

When classification systems or information languages – whether conventional or new – are studied at length, it can be observed that occasionally the control of the terms is carried out a priori, preceding the material or themes as a whole. On other occasions, however, this control or normalisation is carried out by studying the terms – indexing or classification units – themselves, independently of each other but in a reciprocal relationship with one another, according to semantic or generic principles. In other words, it is necessary to consider:

- *pre-controlled languages*;
- *post-controlled languages*.

Examples of the former would be hierarchical classification systems such as the Universal Decimal Classification or faceted classifications such as Ranganathan's Colon Classification. On the other hand, a list of indexing terms or a list of subject headings would be examples of post-controlled information classifications.

Following this line of reasoning, it is now worth considering in which way, or by which means, it is possible to control the terms of an information language. It is again necessary to think of an a priori or prior process, and an a posteriori or subsequent process. This control implies the establishment of hierarchical, associative and equivalence relationships. It will also be necessary to take into account the fact that the terms can be simple or compound, and that the latter can be formed by coordinating its elements, either a priori or a posteriori. It is therefore possible to talk about:

- *pre-coordinated languages* – information languages in which the terms that compose them are coordinated in a process which occurs before they are used. A typical example of this would be a system for subject headings;
- *post-coordinated languages* – information languages in which the terms that the language is composed of are coordinated in a process that happens after they have been selected, for example at the same time as they are established or used. A classic example of this kind of information language would be a thesaurus.

Indexing or information retrieval languages can be pre- or post-coordinated, depending on the requirements of the information system or documentation centre in which they will be used.

From all this we can deduce that a pre-controlled language can be post-coordinated, since this process is carried out in the indexing, classification or information retrieval stages. Consider the following example: someone wants to classify a document on the use of computers in teaching, using the Universal Decimal Classification system (UDC), a pre-controlled system. The themes related to computing and teaching will be found, and they will be combined in such a way as to create a classification appropriate to the document (post-coordination process).

In the specific case of UDC, pre-coordination would imply a pre-control on establishing the hierarchies for its pre-established structure.

On the other hand, a post-controlled information language could be pre-coordinated or post-coordinated, or both, depending on what would be considered to be its construction phase or utilisation phase, both in indexing and information retrieval processes. We could say that a list of (indexing) terms is a post-controlled information language in which the elements comprising the language are coordinated in the phase prior to indexing (pre-coordination) or in a subsequent phase (post-coordination) (see Figure 3.1).

Thesauri

I have purposefully avoided referring to more than one example related to thesauri in the previous section of this work in order to focus on them under their own heading, given their

Figure 3.1   Classes of terminological languages

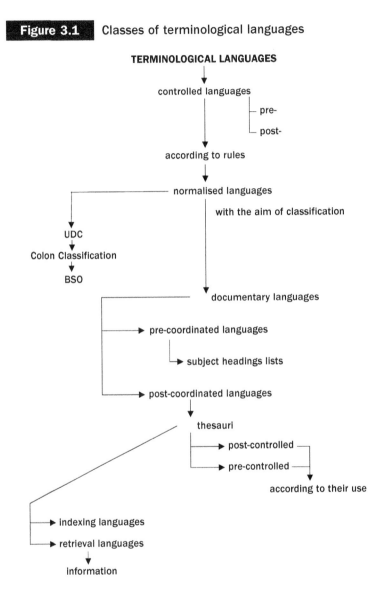

importance in information processes. Nevertheless, some people claim that their glory days are over. New computing methods and, more recently, expert systems in artificial intelligence processes make the use of natural language possible and we do not need to struggle with the complicated subject of the relationships between the terms contained in an information language. This is most definitely becoming the case. However, this will only lighten the workload for users, and possibly the intermediary information professionals who carry out searches for information. Those who develop software programs or make the retrieval of documents possible, the information analysts, no matter how they search a computerised documentation system, they certainly have to know how to establish relationships between terms and coordinate concepts. The intellectual work is not done by machines but by human beings.

We must, therefore, give this topic the importance it deserves, and go on to define what can be understood by the term thesaurus. In the abundant reading which exists on this subject it can be seen that interest in thesauri has grown noticeably in recent years. It is interesting that all information professionals, whether they have a great deal of experience in this area or not, have something to say about thesauri. This tendency is not only evident in Spain; on the contrary, in other countries there also is a clear interest in these classification systems, which in turn are used to develop ontologies or taxonomies (see Figure 3.2).

Thesauri definitions

Let us therefore examine some definitions of thesauri, in order to later study their evolution throughout history and the types of thesauri that are to be found.

In the works I have consulted many different definitions of the word thesaurus can be found. This word has been adapted to the Spanish language, becoming *tesauro*, and its use has become generalised in all Spanish-speaking countries. The word 'thesaurus' comes from a Romanised version of the

Figure 3.2 Development of the concept of the thesaurus

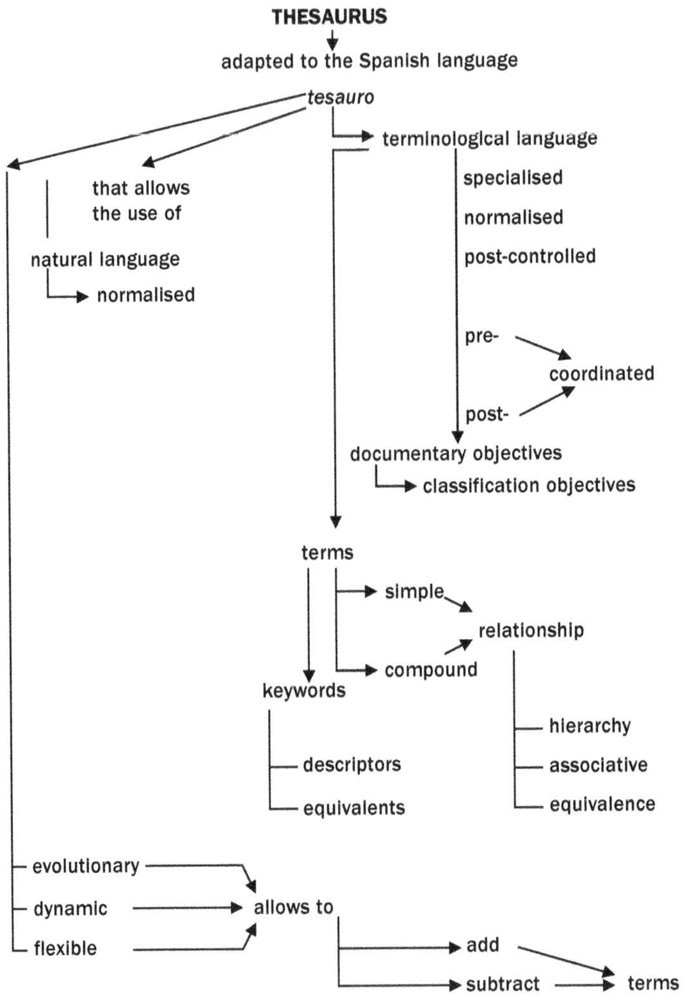

THESAURUS
adapted to the Spanish language
tesauro

terminological language
- specialised
- normalised
- post-controlled

that allows
the use of

natural language
normalised

pre-
post-
coordinated

documentary objectives
classification objectives

terms
- simple
- compound
relationship

keywords

- descriptors
- equivalents

- hierarchy
- associative
- equivalence

- evolutionary
- dynamic
- flexible

allows to

- add
- subtract
terms

Greek expression meaning 'treasury', the place where something valuable is stored.

We shall begin with some definitions of thesaurus that can be found in English and North American dictionaries and which formed the basis for its later use in the field of information science.

The *Shorter Oxford Dictionary* of 1736 defines the term as:

> a treasury or storehouse of knowledge, as a dictionary, encyclopaedia or the like.

In various editions of *Webster's American Dictionary* it is described as:

> a book of words or information about a particular field or set of concepts; especially: a book of words and their synonyms.

In 1852, Peter Mark Roget published his work *Thesaurus of English Words and Phrases*, in which we find a thesaurus defined as:

> a collection of the words it [a language] contains and of the idiomatic combinations peculiar to it, arranged, not in alphabetical order as they are in a Dictionary, but according to the *ideas* which they express.

In other words, when you are dealing with an idea, you must look for the word or words that are most appropriate to that idea. Roget's definition has been the foundation of subsequent meanings and uses of the term thesaurus.

We must now situate ourselves at the end of the 1950s, which is when indexing and classification systems began to be developed and utilised, using keywords as a foundation. One of the first definitions to emerge during those years is that of Howerton, who defines a thesaurus as:

an authorised list that can lead the user to one concept or another by means of heuristic or intuitive relationships. The list can be used manually or mechanically to allocate indexing headings.

Various authors such as Brian Vickery and Alan Gilchrist say that it was Helen Brownson who first used the word thesaurus in print in 1957 during the Dorking Conference on Classification when she wrote:

> The problem [of information retrieval] ... is to transform concepts and their relationships, as expressed in the language of documents, into a somewhat more regularized language, with synonyms controlled and syntactical structures simplified.

Let us now move on and situate ourselves at the start of the 1970s. In 1971, two important works emerged: one in the United Kingdom, written by Alan Gilchrist, and another in Germany, by Gernot Wersig. Both focus on the construction of thesauri. Wersig's book includes a detailed study of the theoretical principles involved in this field, giving rise to a whole *theory of thesauri*. These two publications have been the basis for the majority of subsequent studies.

Gilchrist writes:

> [A thesaurus is] an authorized list of lexis, without notation, which differs from a subject headings list in which the lexical units, being smaller, are more manageable and are used in coordinated indexing.

The same author, in the fourth edition of his book on the construction of thesauri published in 2000, writes:

A thesaurus is a vocabulary of controlled indexing language, formally organized so that, a priori, relationships between concepts are made explicit to be used in information retrieval systems.

Note: We can observe the conceptual changes experienced by this author by comparing the quotations above.

Wersig talks of

lists of terms, predetermined but taken out of the text of documents, which unfold the concepts into simple units. These units are coordinated *a posteriori* in order to avoid ambiguity. Hierarchical, associative and equivalence relationships are established between them.

At that time I started giving classes at the Universidad Autónoma de Madrid (the Autonomous University of Madrid), and I cannot resist giving a definition of a thesaurus that is highly intuitive and appropriate for introducing university students to the topic of thesauri:

specialised vocabulary whose words are semantically and syntactically related to each other.

It goes without saying that it will be necessary later to explain how these relationships are established and the way in which they are used.

In 1976, UNESCO published manuals within the UNISIST programme in which thesauri are defined according to their function and structure:

- *according to function*: they are an instrument for terminological control, used to transfer the descriptors from the natural language used in documents to a linguistic system;

- *according to structure*: they are controlled and dynamic vocabularies of terms that are semantically and generically related, which cover a specific domain of knowledge.

In multilingual thesauri the concepts are represented in more than one language.

In order to better understand the changes that have occurred due to the coming together of Information Science and this terminology, it is useful to look at the definition proposed by Long which appeared in 1980 and was a landmark in the study of the theory of thesauri:

> [A thesaurus] is a semiological whole, used as a classification system, in which the classification units form morpheme groups, linked by paradigmatic relationships, on which the different classes are constructed. These morphemes use syntactic relationships in order to ensure that the terms have an information representation. The relationships between themes are the important thing, rather than the documents. This task is carried out by the indexer. (Cited in Boch de Doze, 1986)

Another definition will now be cited that has also been an important landmark as it comes from a terminologist, the Austrian Helmut Felber. It deals with thesauri from the perspective of terminology in his *Terminology Manual* of 1984, in which he differentiates between vocabulary, dictionaries and 'documentation thesauri'. Of the latter he says that they consist of

> elements – terminological data – that, on the one hand help to control a specific indexing language, and on the other, indicate the relationships between concepts.

In the last few years, various publications, books, lecture notes and manuals have emerged in which definitions of thesauri can be found and which are worth mentioning for their clarity.

In regulation ISO 2788 (British Standard 2733 for thesauri construction) in its second edition from 1986, a thesaurus is defined, among other things, as being 'a vocabulary of a controlled indexing language'. This implies a series of terms extracted from natural language and used to represent, in brief, the themes of documents and which is organised formally with the aim of making the a priori relationships between concepts explicit (for example, 'more generic than' or 'more specific than').

I would also like to include in this list of definitions one that I have used in my courses, which follows the general evolutionary line:

> [It is] a specialised, normalised, post-coordinated language, used with information aims, where the linguistic elements that it is made up of – simple or compound terms – can be related syntactically and semantically.

The definition that appears in the book *Grundlangen der praktischen Information und Dokumentation* (Kuhlen et al., 2004) refers to the classic, well-known definition of a thesaurus as a codified language, taken from natural language, in which each word is accompanied by signs of hierarchical, synonymical and associative relationships.

In the most recent publications, mainly in academic papers and papers presented at conferences or talks etc., definitions of thesauri are presented that, in general, have so far not differed in ideas or concepts from those represented here. An example will now be cited which appeared in the book *Manual de investigación bibliográfica y documental: Teoría y práctica* (*Manual of Bibliographical and Documental Investigation: Theory and Practice*) (Cordón et al., 2001) where we can read that:

- from the point of view of its structure, it is a controlled and dynamic vocabulary of terms that share semantic and generic relationships, and that are applied in a particular field of knowledge;

- from a functional point of view, it is an instrument for the control of terminology, used to transmit, in a more strict language, the language used in documents.

Also recently, in publications dedicated to ontologies and taxonomies and related to the use of computer programs, we can find tentative references to thesauri, always seen through the prism of electronic technology.

Conditions that a thesaurus must fulfil

From the definitions of thesauri mentioned up to this point, whether classic or recent, we can deduce that, in order for a work to be considered a thesaurus, it must fulfil the following conditions:

- It must be a specialised language.

- It must be normalised in a post-controlled process.

- The linguistic units of which it consists, since they are lexis dedicated to a particular theme, acquire the category of terms converted into *keywords*, by which means the theme of the document can be determined.

- These keywords are related to each other hierarchically, in an associative way or by equivalence relationships.

- These relationship processes can be carried out by means of:
  - pre-coordination;
  - post-coordination.
- The languages are terminological, used for information purposes, for which reason they become *information languages* used in:
  - indexing or classification processes;
  - information retrieval processes.
- They must allow the introduction or suppression of terms in order to be constantly updated.
- They must serve for the conversion of the natural, ambiguous, free language of documents into a concrete, normalised language that is appropriate for the control of the information contained in documents.
- They must serve as a nexus of union between the document and the user, where the information professional is a fundamental link.

If the different points are analysed, it is clear that all of them can be reduced to simple rules explained in more or less detail.

It is necessary to study the way in which the relationships between terms and their composition are established. It gives the impression that natural languages have become smaller somehow. I have already commented that we have more ideas than words with which to express them. As will be demonstrated, formulating some rules gives a solution to this problem.

Historical evolution

It is always useful to study the evolution throughout history of the themes being dealt with in order to better comprehend how they have developed and changed over time and to understand the current situation, which, naturally, is not an ending but an intermediate stage and, like all the others, susceptible to future changes and modifications.

With regard to the so-called 'theory of thesauri', everything started with the increase in the themes, both old and new, that emerged in the ever-expanding literature on this subject: the hierarchical or faceted systems did not provide adequate responses to the demand for information. Libraries and documentation centres became obsolete and underused, and therefore suffered corresponding economic losses. A solution had to be found.

That solution came from those who thought that the problem lay with finding or creating new classification systems that would allow for more flexibility in the treatment of the themes contained in documents. Likewise, it was thought that the alphabetical ordering of these themes left gaps in the process of interchanging their relationships. People looked back over the past, focusing on documents that presented systematic structures in the ordering of the concepts that they housed. Carrión mentions the *Libro de los Epítomes* (*The Book of Epitomes*) and *El Libro de Materias o Proposiciones* (*The Book of Materials or Propositions*), both written by Hernando Colón, and the *Dictionarium Historicum* by Charles Estienne, published in 1561, in which systematic classifications were a feature. In this work we have also mentioned documents being ordered in this way. This was not a new idea: it was already in use, but what was missing was finding out whether it could be applied to information processes. So the first classification methods emerged using concepts taken from existing documents that were not necessarily related to each other. They were called thesauri, and they dealt with definitions and documents that also already existed, some of which we have already mentioned in this chapter.

It seems that it all began in recent times, in the mid-1950s, when Howerton and Brownson each independently used the word thesaurus for the first time. This fact coincided with the development of the Uniterm System created by Mortimer Taube which appeared in 1951. In this system the terms, which determined the concepts, were simple linguistic units. According to the available literature on this subject, he was the first person who used the term *keyword* to denote those words that determined the contents of documents. He established categories of keywords. There were main keywords, which were actually used, and other words which were their synonyms. The main keywords were given the name *descriptors* and in this way Taube coined this term for posterity.

Since at that time electronic computers were also beginning to be used, isolated classification units were not that difficult to create. In the process of searching for information, the concepts could be combined using the Boolean system and the desired information could be obtained. The expression *information retrieval* is also attributed to Taube, and it is another term that has passed into general use. The 'Uniterm System' is still used today in great institutions with a considerable volume and a large variety of documents and themes.

That system did not satisfy the majority, however, above all those who managed very specific themes and a smaller volume of documents. This is the reason why Calvin N. Moores, according to available sources, made his Zator system public in 1949, in which the keywords could be simple or compound terms. In this way it became possible to combine the two in the construction phase of the classification system. Moores went on to call his system of index cards, once appropriately produced and prepared, Zatocoding.

Descriptors were used to construct indexes, and so the term *index* was used to denominate the process of obtaining the words from documents that would be used to create indexes. The exact date when this expression began to be used is not known. It must have been before 1945, because in references to faceted classifications the term indexing was already being used.

The following years, roughly between 1947 and 1960, were times of great activity in the settlement of theoretical principles and the definition of different processes.

In some cases the existing data is contradictory, and it is difficult to know exactly what happened and at what time. We have said that Howerton and Brownson were the first to offer a definition of a thesaurus. In other publications this honour is attributed to Joyce and Neddham in 1956; it is also said that it was Farradane, writing in 1952, who first mentioned this term.

In other works the use of the term 'coordinated indexing' is attributed to Taube, although the date comes towards the end of the 1950s. There is another reference in a book by Gilchrist which says that Jolley defined 'pre-coordinated indexing' in 1963. Knowing the exact date is not of the utmost importance. What is important is to follow the evolution that has occurred over time, and that the documents published on this subject over the years are recognised.

Naturally, in those early years people aimed to define the basic theories and concepts involved. Thus, at the time we have mentioned, the concepts of descriptor, indexing, coordinated indexing, relevance, pertinence and so on were defined. A great concern for constructing a system that might determine the contents of documents is evident.

The first formally constructed thesauri appear from 1960 onwards. The thesaurus of the Armed Service Technical Information Agency (ASTIA) – which later became known as the Defense Documentation Center (DDC) – was published in 1960. Thus began an era in which the main concern was the construction of thesauri. Nevertheless, this age does not stand out for its excessive activity in this field. It is in the following decade, the 1970s, that a flurry of events can be noticed which continued to put an emphasis on the construction of thesauri. It has been observed that the interest in thesauri has had a marked tendency to emphasise their usefulness in information retrieval. This tendency has not yet entered a decline.

Between 1969 and 1970 the Preserved Context Indexing System (PRECIS) was published, which has been the guiding document in the development of the British Library system. In 1971, the works of Gilchrist and Wersig emerged.

Before this, in 1967, a work group had been formed in Germany for the construction of a thesaurus for the chemicals industry, in which I had the pleasure of participating.

The 'TEST' or 'Thesaurus of Engineering and Scientific Terms' was published in 1967, and was used as the basis for British Standard 5723 for thesaurus construction. Likewise, ISO used this document as a model for the creation of ISO 2788, in its first edition in 1974.

The fact that the field of computing developed, and that computers became more and more available on the market and easier to use, promoted the automatisation of information sciences. This was the reason for the boom in the field of thesauri. This could be seen not only in more or less industrialised countries, but also worldwide. South America deserves a mention because of its cultural proximity to Spain; the work carried out in Chile, Colombia, Venezuela, Argentina and Brazil can be highlighted.

Many works were published in the 1970s, and also in the following decade. From that time on the necessity of having effective thesauri available has been ever present, both for indexing and information retrieval purposes. Nowadays computers are more affordable and easier to use, and so attention is focused on the user. The most relevant works are based on the works of Fugmann, Lancaster, Snow, Sievert and Boyce, and Foskkett, among others, who are well known in this field.

With the emergence of ontologies and taxonomies, more definitions of thesauri have appeared in the last few years: from 2003, the works of Gilchrist, Pastor and Diego Ferreira, among others, are worth mentioning.

In 2004, various other publications emerged. Those worth a mention include those by Kuhlen et al., Schuff et al., Krumholz, Bauer and Wiggins, who again are all well known authors in this field.

Note: As a general comment, the number of publications that have appeared over the last few years is in itself striking.

With regard to theoretical studies, there is a tendency to combine them with terminology and linguistics. Ontologies and taxonomies are also often included.

Classes of thesauri

Having dealt with the definitions of thesauri and highlighted the general characteristics that they must have, we will now spend some time studying classes and kinds of thesauri.

We know that one of the principal characteristics of a thesaurus is that it is based on a specialised theme. However, some thesauri deal with a general field and therefore an initial classification might be (as shown in Figure 3.3):

- general thesauri;
- specialised thesauri.

Despite the specialisation of a thesaurus, it can cover more than one discipline with different levels of importance. Of course, general thesauri are by definition multidisciplinary. Therefore another classification that could be established is:

Figure 3.3   Classes of thesauri

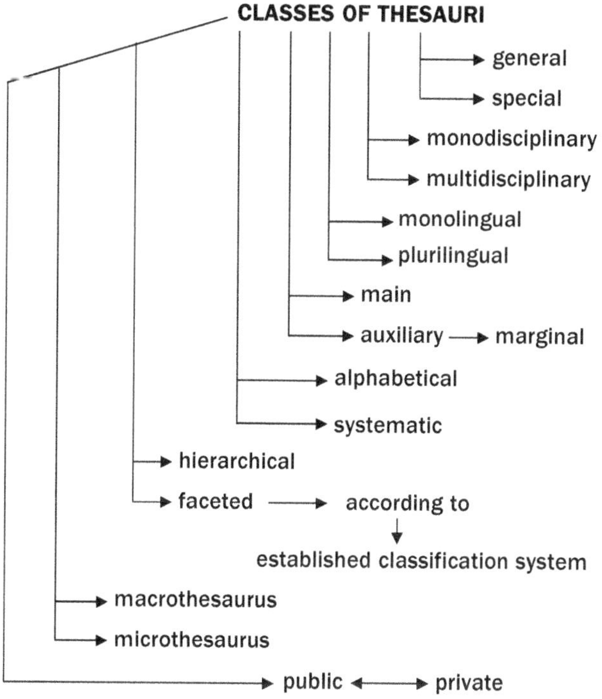

CLASSES OF THESAURI

- general
- special
- monodisciplinary
- multidisciplinary
- monolingual
- plurilingual
- main
- auxiliary → marginal
- alphabetical
- systematic
- hierarchical
- faceted → according to
  ↓
  established classification system
- macrothesaurus
- microthesaurus
- public ←→ private

- multidisciplinary thesauri; and
- monodisciplinary thesauri.

It is clear that it is very difficult to use a strictly monodisciplinary thesaurus.

Some marginal themes are always included that coincide with the main theme. For this reason, when using a main thesaurus it is often necessary to use another one to support it. Therefore there are:

- main thesauri; and
- marginal or auxiliary thesauri.

This depends on the field or theme which they encompass.

When we consider the position of the theme or themes being dealt with, the classifications become more diverse. We know that one of the main characteristics of a thesaurus is its simplicity with regard to the relationships between its terms. It would seem, therefore, that an alphabetical ordering of keywords would be the best way of ordering its thematic material. Nevertheless, experience has demonstrated that, in the majority of cases, a systematic ordering is necessary and useful. Consequently, it is necessary to think about:

- alphabetic thesauri;
- systematic thesauri, which are also known as thematic thesauri.

In systematic thesauri the materials that they contain can be ordered in a hierarchy, distributed in facets or depicted by graphics where appropriate. We can conclude from this that thesauri can be:

- hierarchical;
- faceted;
- graphic.

The majority of thesauri present a structure that is:

- alphabetic;
- systematic;
- graphic.

From the moment that the use of computers became generalised, the management of thesauri became much easier and faster, which has meant that the graphic ordering of terms within thesauri has begun to disappear. It is necessary to take into account the fact that their development is a laborious and time-consuming task, and that they are not particularly useful, given that in any case an alphabetic list is required in order to locate keywords.

It is now also worth mentioning two other kinds of thesauri:

- macrothesauri;
- microthesauri.

A *macrothesaurus* is a thesaurus that contains themes that are related to each other but located in different sections, as if it were a collection of various smaller thesauri. In fact, this is exactly what it is. A macrothesaurus consists of various microthesauri which are related to each other by cross references, and that include a wide variety of themes, each one being the subject of a specialised microthesaurus. These can be detached from the macrothesaurus and constitute individual thesauri in their own right. Some classic examples of macrothesauri are OCDE and CLADES.

It is still worth mentioning the languages in which the terms contained in a thesaurus can be written, it being possible to find thesauri that are:

- monolingual;
- bilingual;
- plurilingual.

They can play an important role in translation work as auxiliary dictionaries.

If we focus on the entity that creates a thesaurus, we must take into account that this entity might be:

- public;
- private.

It is necessary to take into account whether a thesaurus was created with public or private funds, and whether it is affordable or not.

In all countries there are offices or official institutions that are in charge of such matters as the creation of rules, for example the Asociación Española para Normalización (AENOR) in Spain and the British Standards in the United Kingdom.

The reader is recommended to visit such offices or institutions in order to obtain information on the rules concerning the field of information sciences.

Topics for discussion

1. How would you define a thesaurus?

2. What is your opinion of the usefulness of a thesaurus?

3. What is the difference between an indexing process and a classification process?

4. What do you think a descriptor is?

5. Give an example of a characteristic exclusive to thesauri.

6. What is a terminological language?

7. What is the difference between a controlled language and a coordinated language?

8. What is the difference between a hierarchical thesaurus and a thematic thesaurus?

9. When should you use the expression 'term' and when should you use 'descriptor' in order to denote a linguistic unit of a thesaurus?

References

Aitchison, J., Gilchrist, A. and Bawden, D. (2000) *Thesaurus Construction and Use: A Practical Manual*, 4th edn. London: Aslib IMI.

Boch de Doze, A. (1986) 'Article', *Revista Española de Documentación Científica*, 9 (2): 70.

Burkart, M. (1997) 'Thesauri', in R. Kuhlen, T. Seeger and D. Strauch (eds) *Grundlagen der praktischen Information und Dokumentation*, 5th edn (first published 1972). Munich: K.G. Sauer, pp. 141–5.

Castillo, L. and Cueva, A. de la (2007) 'Evolución y uso de los lenguajes controlados en documentación informativa', *El Profesional de la Información*, 16 (6): 617–26.

Comala, M. (2003) 'La clasificación: una estrategia de comunicación', *VIII Jornadas Españolas de Documentación. FESABID 2003: Los Sistemas de información en las organizaciones: eficacia y transparencia*. Barcelona.

Cordón García, J.A., López Lucas, J. and Vaquero Pulido, J.R. (2001) *Tesauros. Manual de investigación bibliográfica y documental. Teoría y práctica*. Madrid: Ediciones Pirámide.

Currás, E. (1985) *Nuevo método de clasificación. Documentación y metodología de la investigación científica*, cuaderno de trabajo. Madrid: Paraninfo.

Currás, E. (1991) *T(h)esauros. Lenguajes terminológicos*. Madrid: Paraninfo.

Currás, E. (1996) *T(h)esauros. Linguagens terminológicas*. Brasilia: CNPq-IBICT.

García Marco, F.J. (2007) 'Ontologías y organización del conocimiento: retos y oportunidades para el profesional de la información', *El Profesional de la Información*, 16 (6): 541–50.

Gilchrist, A. (1994) 'Classification and thesauri', in B.C. Vickery (ed.), *Fifty Years of Information Progress: A Journal of Documentation Review*. London: Aslib, pp. 85–118.

Gilchrist, A. (2003) 'Structuring vocabularies in enterprise-wide systems', contact: *cura@fastnet.co.uk*.

Kuhlen, R., Seeger, T. and Strauch, D. (eds) (2007) *Grundlagen der praktischen Information und Dokumentation*, 5th edn (first published 1972). Munich: K.G. Sauer.

López-Huertas, J.M. (1997) 'Thesaurus structure design: a conceptual approach for improved interaction', *Journal of Documentation*, 53 (2): 139–77. Online at: *http:// www.aslib.co.uk/*.

Monchón Bezares, G. and Sorli Rojo, A. (2007) 'Tesauros de ciencias sociales en Internet', *Revista Española de Documentación Científica*, 30 (3): 395–419.

Monchón Bezares, G. and Sorli Rojo, A. (2008) 'Tesauros de humanidades en Internet', *Revista Española de Documentación Científica*, 31 (3): 437–52.

Monchón Bezares, G. and Sorli Rojo, A. (2008) 'Tesauros multidisciplinares en Internet', *Revista Española de Documentación Científica*, 31 (3): 129–39.

Pastor Sánchez, J.A. and Martínez Méndez, F.J. (2003) 'Gestión colaborativa de tesaurus en Internet', *Scire*, 9 (1): 85–98.

Pedraza Jiménez, R., Codina, L.L. and Rovira, C. (2007) 'Web semántica y ontologías en el procesamiento de la información documental', *El Profesional de la Información*, 16 (6): 569–78.

Rodríguez Bravo, B. and Alvite Díez, M.L. (2002) *Construcción de un tesauro de Ciencias de la Documentación aplicado a la docencia de las técnicas documentales*. Contact: *dphbrb@unileon.es*.

Sánchez Cuadrado, S., Morato Lara, J., Palacios Madrid, V., Llorens Morillo, J. and Moreira González, J.A. (2007) 'De repente, ¿todos hablamos de ontologías?', *El Profesional de la Información*, 16 (6): 561–8.

Sánchez Jiménez, R. (2007) 'Gil Urdician, B.: Lenguajes documentales y ontologías', *El Profesional de la Información*, 16 (6): 551–60.

Shoman, S. and Kedar, R. (2002) 'The subject cataloguing of monographs with the use of a thesaurus', paper presented at the Seventh International ISKO Conference, Granada, in M.J. López-Huertas (ed.), *Challenges in Knowledge Representation and Organization for the 21st Century: Integration of Knowledge across Boundaries*. Würzburg: Ergon-Verlag, pp. 173–80.

Warner, A.J. (2005) 'Thesaurus design specialist/Information architect'. Contact: *http://www.lexonomy.com*.

Wiggins, R. (2004) *Beyond the Spider: The Accidental Thesaurus*, online at: *http://www.infotoday.com/searcher/oct02/wiggins.htm*.

4

Thesauri in (cladist) systematics

The idea of applying (cladist) systematics to thesaurus construction theory first arose as a way of comparing both classification systems. The aim was to strengthen the scientific nature of thesaurus construction theory, thus positioning it within the accepted canon of knowledge in this area (Currás, 1994).

At the same time, a complementary intention was to apply systematics to branches of knowledge other than logic, mathematics and biology, thus broadening its scope and evolutionary development.

The decision to apply (cladist) systematics rather than any other characteristic or categorising subdivision was inspired by recent discoveries of how information technology can be applied to systematics, or perhaps vice versa (Currás, 1994).

Systematics

The distinctive characteristic of systematics, which has existed since the time of the Greeks, is that it houses a variety of aspects within a whole. The most common use of the term, and the one that is most true to its real meaning, refers to its classificatory nature as a method or way of obtaining classifications – of anything whatsoever.

The word 'systematics' has both an adjectival and a nominal form. It is only in recent years that systematics has come to be considered as being related to information technology.

On performing an Internet search, one finds many more hits for 'systematic' used as an adjective (used in conjunction with a noun, in the context of ordering or classification) than for the noun 'systematics'. References to the noun are almost exclusively in relation to biology. When adding the term 'information technology' to that of 'systematics' in Internet searches, a very small number of references appear, dating from just before the year 2000, in which the classificatory nature of systematics is evident, however, in a rather different sense to its application in biology. These may be attempts to find parallels with taxonomy as used in the area of information technology (see Figure 4.1).

The meaning of the adjective 'systematic', when used in conjunction with a noun or a verb, is to order according to a set method which is logical, consistent, scientific and applicable to what is being ordered (see Figure 4.2).

It is common to speak of systematic classification, systematic categorisation and even 'systematisation' itself.

Returning now to our area of interest, information science and, more specifically, the thesaurus, many works in this category offer a 'systematic representation'.

By way of example, let us consider GEMET: A Multilingual Thesaurus of the Environment (see Currás, 1994). Its systematic representation is organised hierarchically, using a seven-level tree diagram with the terms divided into 27 groups. It is clear from this that this work is ordered according to a pre-established method. The Thesaurus of Computer Networks is another outstanding example of systematic representation using categories that cover a broad spectrum: network architecture and design, data communication, communication protocols, etc. Each of these is divided into subcategories and then into sub-subcategories.

Figure 4.1 Concept of systematics

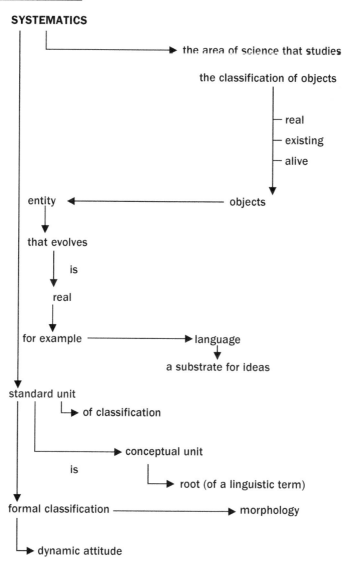

The whole constitutes a formal classification system of the terms that make up this thesaurus. (See Currás, 1994.)

Of the many examples which could be presented, those mentioned above are sufficient to illustrate the point.

Figure 4.2 Systematics as classification method

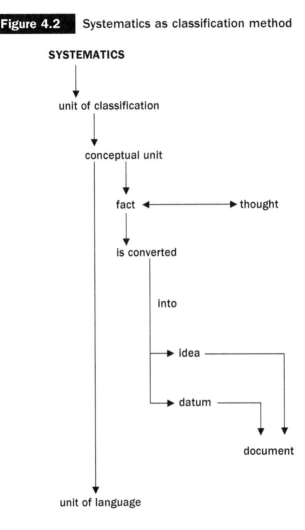

Systematics as a noun

In this work our interest is focused on the discipline of systematics, aiming to urge readers not only to consider systematics as a science in itself, but also its application to the theory of the construction and use of thesauri.

Similarly, in this case, since ancient times, systematics has fallen within the realms of logic and mathematics and has been studied by only a small number of philosophers.

Systematics was made popular by the biologist Carl Linnaeus who, not knowing how to give order to the wide variety of living organisms that he encountered in his studies, decided to borrow from this discipline. He is thought to have used the term in this context for the first time in 1735; however, its use was not formalised until the publication of his work *Systema Naturae* in 1758.

Definitions and historic evolution over time

From that moment on, systematics has been in constant use within the realm of biology. Different scientists have developed or even discovered specific aspects that merit the establishment of new categories and subdivisions.

The word systematic is etymologically derived from the word system, which in turn, according to Plato, is derived from *syn* (= together) and *stesai* (= formal cause). The Espasa Encyclopaedia defines it, within the domain of logic, as 'that part of science that sets out to classify its own objects' and later, more specifically, 'concrete objects'. According to this definition, it appears that only real, existing, live entities may be classified, hence its application in biology.

However, the concept of 'real entity' and even the concepts of 'existing' or 'living entity' require further explanation. A living being is one which has the capacity to evolve, transform or change. Does language, the substrate for all our ideas, not evolve, transform or change? Could language be considered a living entity? The answer to this question appears obvious. The conceptual unit itself also evolves and is alive inasmuch as it is born in the human brain, which is itself continually evolving towards improved capacity and perfection. By this line of reasoning, systematics can also be applied to linguistics, terminology and, as a consequence, information science.

Other erudite scientists, such as Goethe, found a similarity with morphology as a study of form. The German scientists Baer, Neckel and Oken refined this idea further, ending up with idealistic morphology.

Systematics became an incontestable part of biology from the moment that Charles Darwin presented his theory of evolution (1859), postulating that one organism could give rise to others and taking as his example a branched tree. In his work *The Origin of Species* published in 1859, he proposed his 'own evolutionary mechanism'. From this point on, biology experienced its own boom, with more and more biologists working on the evolution of the species, not to mention the 'creationists' that also appeared, opposed to evolution.

- Systematics can therefore be defined as the science of diversity, or the science of the organisation of all existing knowledge about organisms. It includes phylogenetic information (of the species) and taxonomic information (of the individual).

- It can also be defined as a synthesising discipline, involving the abstraction of concepts and the enunciation of theories to explain observed phenomena. It thus has a much greater underlying empirical, theoretical nature than that of taxonomy, as well as a vocation to predict the future.

- Hartwig, agreeing with Azorín, said that systematics is born out of comparing individuals – isolated entities – and noticing their differences in characteristics and features.

- Alvarado Ballester's description considers that the greater the number of characteristics taken into consideration, the greater the information content about that group. Parallels can be noted with the technique of indexing, in the sense that the greater the number of descriptors taken from the text, the more accurate it will be.

In systematics the subjective aspect is eliminated, as it considers the formal characteristics of the objects intended for classification. There is no room for interpretation. Nor in thesaurus theory, when carrying out searches for example, is there room for interpretation; either a descriptor is obtained or it is not. In reality, it is not always possible to be quite that restrictive.

Systematics does nonetheless have an evolutionary component; in fact, this is one of its most distinguishing characteristics.

Differences between taxonomy and systematics

Given the obvious similarities between taxonomy and systematics, identifying the differences comes as no easy task. This, however, would seem an appropriate moment to attempt to do so.

Not even the specialists express clear ideas on this matter. In taxonomy the most common opinion is that classification is performed a priori, with systematics performing this classification in a more formal manner. This 'explanation' does not seem to clarify the matter.

The document 'Systematics and Taxonomy' states that 'the establishment of classification principles corresponds to a discipline named systematics, which includes the study of the taxonomic classification principles', also failing to shed much light on the issue.

Summarising the references on the subject, it could be said that in taxonomy, formal classification criteria are applied. Their consolidation is the domain of systematics. Taxonomy is static, whereas systematics is dynamic, as was noted by Leclerc.

In taxonomy the criterion used to select the taxa and the relationships between them is influenced by a determining factor of subjectivity located in the classifying agent. In systematics, this subjectivity is eliminated by taking into account the formal, preferably real, characteristics of the basic units of what is being classified and their likewise formal relationships.

Taxonomy sets classification criteria with objects (individuals, species or groups of species) being grouped into categories on the basis of the properties of the objects that are being classified. This is an eminently empirical and descriptive way of organising (biological) information, which operates by accumulating phenomena, facts and objects, which it uses to generate the primary hypotheses to explain the ordering mechanism. Systematics performs this ordering process in a formal manner, i.e. taxonomically. Perhaps it should not be quite so rigorous.

Systematics in thesaurus construction theory

We will now return to the meaning of the word systematics to consider some of the other definitions found in the literature that, like those mentioned above, will serve as a basis for our reasoning process and help to fit systematics into thesaurus theory.

In systematics one has to decide on the standard classification unit, which does not necessarily have to be the most simple or indivisible part, nor the most complete. In fact, in biology, species is often used as a classification unit.

In thesaurus construction theory, one could also take as the standard basic unit for organising one's systematics the root of a word, ignoring the various endings, prefixes and suffixes. In fact, this is precisely what occurs in the documentary languages processed by computers, in which words are truncated in order to be able to search using the root.

Alvarado Ballester (2000) writes that 'the progress of systematics results in an ordered representation of living beings, which is formalised using a classification system ...' This work aims to generalise and extrapolate this statement, by substituting the term conceptual units for living beings, from which we derive information units and units of useful information.

Each of these units, in turn, will be utilised to make up the basic systematic units to be used for their classification. From this point on, the words 'individuals', 'living beings' and 'species' will be substituted by 'conceptual', or 'information units', according to context.

Systematics could now be applied to information science in the area of thesaurus construction theory.

Those researchers that came after Darwin, such as Genermont, Sachs and Florkin, consider that in systematics it is necessary to take into account an evolutionary component, principally determined by the brain's capacity to evolve on receiving information from the outside, which has an impact on the information units within the brain itself, affecting its development and behaviour.

For biologists, these information units are located in the genes, which evolve according to phylogenetic information;

some even go so far as to want to measure them in bits. Such measurements would apparently be extremely difficult in the present day, since the brain of a normal adult may have somewhere between 50,000 and 80,000 million neurons.

This leads us to consider the great potential for development of the human brain and to predict that humans in the future will have a far greater capacity for intelligence, learning and investigation, leading to inventions and discoveries that are currently unimaginable.

For now, the human brain must continue to develop in order to assimilate all the information that it receives. It performs this process by using systematics to devise and create classification methods to order its ideas and attitudes to life.

According to Adamson and Vicq d'Azyr, a well ordered systematics has a large number of characteristics in order to determine the position and order of each of the systematic units and the relationships between them. 'It seems obvious', writes Alvarado Ballester (2000), 'that the more characteristics are used, the greater the information content for the group.' These statements fit well into the context of information science, since the greater the number of characteristics present, for example in a document, the more effective its identification and location.

It seems to follow that systematics not only may be applied to the context of information science, but that it should in fact be an integral element of this discipline. We shall not categorise it as 'aristocience', in the style of Teilhard de Chardin and Martin Municio when they linked them to aristobiology; nevertheless, it can be affirmed that it forms a primordial component in its development. It appears obvious that without order and classification it would be impossible to dominate the vast world of ideas that are the principal focus of information science.

Classic, numerical and cladist systematics

From current studies of systematics the following divisions can be deduced:

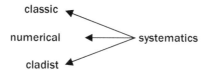

Likewise, other scientists use the following categories:

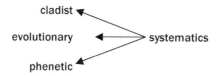

For the purpose of this work the first set of categories is the most adequate, being the most suited to be applied to thesauri construction and use theory.

We started from the principle that the units chosen as the basic building blocks for systematics are those known as *systematic units*. In the case of information science, these would be the *conceptual units* derived from the fact which may be:

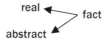

and which, by predicating its existence on a historical context and a tangible medium, successively becomes:

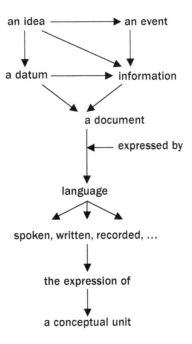

By means of clear reasoning the following units will be identified:

- conceptual unit
- unit of language

contained in documents. These units will be used as the basis for our successive studies of systematics.

Now is the point at which to look at what relationship there may be between classic, numerical and cladist systematics and thesaurus construction theory.

Classic systematics in information science

Classic systematics, which has also been called typological systematics, experienced a boom with Linnaeus. Until the time of Darwin it was only descriptive and was engaged in determining the characteristics of the entities to be classified by fixing their properties.

In information science it would set, on the one hand, *the forms of language*, and on the other hand, *the forms of documents*. It would have a double mission and would draw from bibliography, archivistics, information science in general and linguistics (see Figure 4.3).

After Darwin published his theories, 'an evolutionary component' was introduced, which would require us, in our case, to take into account comparative linguistics and philology studies and to introduce both historical and neurophysiological correction factors. The evolution of documents and of language throughout history must be taken into consideration in order to achieve more accurate classification.

The great, pre-coordinated universal classification systems could be included within classic systematics, such as Amenope's

Figure 4.3   Classic systematics

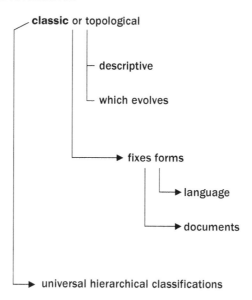

SYSTEMATICS

classic or topological

— descriptive

— which evolves

→ fixes forms

→ language

→ documents

→ universal hierarchical classifications

and Avicenna's classification systems or those by Raimundus Lullus in his *Ars Magna* and Juan Huarte in his *Examination of Men's Wits for the Sciences*, and likewise the Dewey Decimal Classification system, the Universal Decimal Classification and those of the Library of Congress or UNESCO, etc.

All these are methods within systematics that can be used to classify both ideas and documents (see Figure 4.3).

Numerical systematics in information science

Numerical systematics was developed in North America, well into the twentieth century, by Sokal and Sneath. These scientists highlighted the difficulties that classic systematics has in classifying certain 'individuals' due to the small number of characteristics that are taken into consideration.

The scope of human knowledge had grown to such an extent and such a large number of discoveries had been made within the animal and plant kingdoms, in particular by using new instruments and powerful apparatuses, that biologists were unsure as to how to set up a suitable classification system.

The solution appeared to lie in increasing the number of characteristics in order to make the method more accurate. Likewise, it would be necessary to start with a large number of individual objects which would need to be ordered methodically for improved data manipulation and handling. A numeric code would also be required in order to evaluate the characteristic and later perform the corresponding mathematical and statistical operations. These days it does not matter how complex these mathematical and statistical operations are, given the high speed at which computers work.

When a large number of characteristics is set, the number of subdivisions to be taken into consideration increases and a simpler element is taken as the systematic unit with sets of similar characteristics then being established. Each of these sets forms an *OTU* (*operational taxonomic unit*).

Studies on the similarities and the dissimilarities between the different OTUs allow us to establish 'association' and 'correlation coefficients' or 'systematic distances'.

Applying these concepts to information science, surprising parallels can be observed between the two branches of human knowledge, information science and biology. Naturally, general phenomena have occurred among humankind that have affected all the sciences without exception, such as the industrial explosion, the huge increase in knowledge, the unchecked spread of information, etc. (see Figure 4.4).

Figure 4.4   Numerical systematics

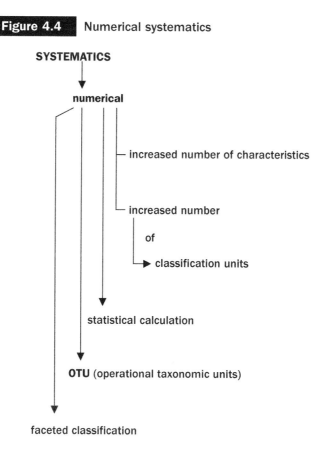

Information Science found its classic methods insufficient to denominate and classify documents, ideas or information. A greater quantity of identification data was required, with relationships being established between them. It was also necessary to be more specific or specialised, and to break down the materials that were being classified even further. The same characters as before were also established horizontally between the units being classified.

It was necessary to devise and organise *faceted* classifications, ordered by *facets*, *categories* and *families*.

The smallest unit of classification is the word itself, the expression of a concept, and complicated numerical notations and devices are used in order to classify concepts, ideas and data as well as the documents containing them.

Here the OTUs are composed specifically of facets formed by words considered to be facets at a horizontal level with regard to their conceptual content.

These OTUs are the information bearers that carry the receiving agent and to which an evaluation factor is assigned and for which a weighted scale is established.

Faceted classifications thus fit within numerical systematics.

Thesauri in cladist systematics

It has been necessary to delve a long way into the background before being able to relate systematics, and specifically its most relevant type, *cladist systematics*, to thesauri. This has been the most studied branch of systematics and, over time, it has come to be considered a discipline all of its own named cladism or cladistics by Christoffersen in 1995.

Cladist systematics was described by W. Henning in 1950 and revised in 1965 and again in 1966 after he had identified imperfections in the classification method when applied to a group of insects. It involves a greater degree of complexity within systematics itself.

Knowledge continued to increase, with more and more animal and plant species appearing which required classification. A greater degree of specificity was required, with the individual animal or plant not being of interest so much as its characteristics, which continued to grow in importance.

Henning thus brought the level of specification down to that of the characteristics of individuals, which led him to consider structural units as the carriers of the minimum possible amount of information. He called these units *semaphoronts*, meaning 'bearers of information units'. This designation appeals to us as being absolutely perfect for use within the context of information theory (see Figure 4.5).

Figure 4.5 Cladist systematics

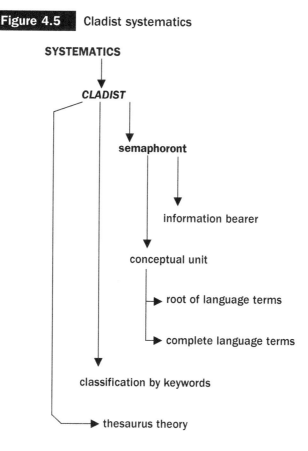

The meaning of semaphoront is more restrictive than that of individual, being able to refer to only one phase of the life cycle. The semaphoront therefore becomes the *basic unit of classification* which in our case is expressed by the:

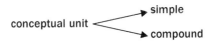

that carries information, also expressed by a *word* or set of words.

Words will therefore always be bearers of *useful information*, for which reason they become keywords ... *descriptors* which are not always made up of single terms.

In cladistics, the basic classification unit is called the *clade*. The same logic is applied to the clade as to the semaphoront, for which reason the clade becomes a *descriptor*. Semaphoronts are related to other semaphoronts by means of certain shared features such as the *derived character*, giving rise to 'apomorphy' or the primitive character corresponding to 'plesiomorphy'.

For the purpose of this work, the derived character will be understood as the establishment of a hierarchical dependency of the semaphoronts or descriptors with a broad scope of content, starting with a higher unit with a comprehensive meaning and descending to the most simple unit, forming families, in other words taking the umbrella term, generic term, specific term, etc., e.g. ocean, sea, cove, bay, etc.

When the characters have similar 'apomorphies', the term *sister groups* is used for those descendants of a common ancestor. The sister groups with a shared ancestor would be composed, in our case, of *synonymous keywords*.

The primitive character would refer to those terms that are derived from a shared branch. In the case of thesauri, one would include truncated words composed of a shared root and certain suffixes and prefixes to complete the meaning of the term.

By way of example, let us take the root 'electri':

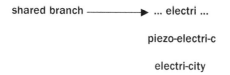

On the basis of this reasoning and a study of all these types of term, drawn from the construction and use of thesauri and comparable to the types of semaphoront formed in cladist systematics, it can be concluded that the latter is perfectly applicable to thesaurus theory and that in fact thesauri constitute a part of cladist systematics.

Up to this point, it has been demonstrated that some disciplines, along with their theoretical/practical principles, which are at the basis of taxonomy and systematics and that in the past have been closely and almost exclusively linked to biology, may be applied to other sciences as distinct in their content and concepts as Information Science.

Nowadays, the sciences have become more universal, and they are no longer isolated from one another.

Systematics in information technology

Systematics offers two different aspects for use in this domain. Firstly, it should be considered in its primary meaning as the categorisation or ordering of what is to be classified. Secondly, it is used also to classify, but in this case with its own specific method, structured in facets, which attempts to embrace the full scope of the domain to which it is being applied. In the latter case there are strong parallels with the taxonomy that we have called 'computing taxonomy', as discussed in Chapter 2.

One could also talk about systematics applied to information technology and vice versa, i.e. information technology applied to systematics. With regard to the two meanings mentioned above, the first would involve the application of systematics to information technology, while in the second, information technology is applied to systematics.

In both cases, a computer application is involved, with proper software being developed. The dates of the references found in Internet searches are interesting, with the oldest reference dating from 1998 and most having been created during the twenty-first century.

Some examples

To illustrate the above, some examples are presented below.

For the purposes of this work, it will be more interesting to consider those examples in which a specific systematics has been developed, and later to search for the computer methods, software designs, etc. required to complete them.

- GEMET: A Multilingual Thesaurus of the Environment is the most interesting from our point of view as professionals, as it offers a computer application, known as THESshow, which makes it possible to browse the GEMET Thesaurus to search for the appropriate terms for indexing or retrieving documents. This could be used in libraries or environmental information centres.

- Another example in which systematics is used to represent a type of classification using information technology is the Excite Spain Economy Directory, where a computer application has been developed for the systematic interpretation of the economy.

- Likewise, in the 2nd World Congress on Law and Information Technology in 2002, mention was made of systematic action with reference to information technology for law.

All the following examples (in chronological order) refer to companies needing to categorise their documents originating on both their intranet and extranet but with an external focus for productive and financial purposes. In all cases a faceted method has been created for ordering the products they handle, produce or offer.

- The software engineering company Sistematica established the following main categories: Companies, Members, Contacts, Development, Software, Hardware, Services.

- Inforsalud 99, the 3rd National Congress on Health Informatics, used the following primary descriptor families: Confirm Diagnosis, Refuse Diagnosis, Periodic Surveillance, Case Follow-up.

- The Italian company Sistematica, srl, founded in 2002 and dedicated to software engineering for management information technology, uses the following basic categories: Intranet, Extranet, Companies, Representatives Abroad, and then draws up a list of the countries in which they have branches or representatives.

- Also, Omesa Informática, sl, established in 2002 and located in Palencia (Spain), is dedicated principally to the automotive industry and organises its information using the following modules: Administration, Spare Parts, Workshop, Sales.

All these cases show the variety of needs of entities or companies in relation to the ordering and classifying of their documents. Each one, depending on its characteristics, purposes and aims, has derived its own classes or categories to organise the documents that they handle. There are no norms or rules. Nothing is set in stone.

To search the relationships that may exist between these different types of categorisation and the construction and use of thesauri is of great interest for the purpose of this work. On first view, they appear to be different systems, since in one case faceted classifications may be formed and in another hierarchical classifications grouped into families. But therein may lie the similarity as the families form horizontal platforms between themselves that are indeed ... faceted. In the examples mentioned only the main categories are given, which function as umbrella terms later divided into subcategories and sub-subcategories, etc., in a hierarchical structure. Both cases refer to the theory of construction and use of thesauri.

Before finishing this chapter, let us remember that the use of systematics in information technology has only just begun. It may come to supplant taxonomy or it may pursue a parallel evolutionary path, but whatever the case it is a topic that should be pursued in the future.

Topics for discussion

1. Do you agree that taxonomy may be applied to information science?

2. Could you explain what you understand by systematics?

3. Could you explain the differences between taxonomy and systematics?

4. Do you think that a system of keywords could be considered a method of classification within classic systematics?

5. Do you believe that an idea may be a 'semaphoront'?

6. Does it seem appropriate to you to use the term 'semaphoront' to describe a conceptual unit?

7. Do you think that an information unit is the same as a conceptual unit?

8. What differences do you find between classic systematics and cladist systematics?

9. Where would you place the Universal Decimal Classification: in classic, numerical or cladist systematics?

10. Where would you place faceted classification?

References

Adamson and Vicq d'Azyr, cited in Alvarado Ballester, R. (1967) *Sistemática, taxonomía, clasificación y nomenclatura*, Lecture. Madrid: Ed. Universidad de Madrid, Facultad de Ciencias.

Alvarado Ballester, R. (2000) *Comunicación, información, evolución biológica*. Lecture. Madrid: Instituto de España.

Currás, E. (1988) 'Taxonomía y sistemática', *La Información en sus Nuevos Aspectos*. Madrid: Paraninfo, pp. 170–92.

Currás, E. (1994) *An Approach to the Application of Sistematics to Knowledge Organization*. 47th FID Conference and Congress: 'Finding New Values and Uses of Information', Sonic City, Omiya, Saitama (Japan).

Currás, E. (1996) *Dialectic Information Systems and Its Connection with the New Economy*. 48th FID Conference and Congress: 'Globalization. The Networking Information Society', Graz, October 1996, in FID (ed.) (1998) *Proceedings*. The Hague: FID, pp. 61–8.

Leclerc de Buffon, G.L. (1828) *Histoire naturelle, générale et particulière*. Paris, 1828; also cited in Alvarado Ballester, R. (1967) *Sistemática, taxonomía, clasificación y nomenclatura*, Lecture. Madrid: Instituto de España.

'Presentación Sistemática del Tesauro' (2006) Online at: *http://www.um.es/gtiweb/fjmm/tesauro/sistematica.htm*.

Sokal, R.R. and Sneath, P.H.A. (1963) *Principles of Numerical Taxonomy*. San Francisco: W.H. Freeman.

'Systematics and taxonomy', cited in Alvarado Ballester, R. (2000), *Comunicación, información, evolución biológica*, Lecture. Madrid: Instituto de España.

5

Thesauri in systems theory

Today, human knowledge has evolved at such a rate in modern times that its fields of action have expanded, meaning that we can no longer think of a single human activity as isolated in its own field. Individuals are no longer isolated entities in nature, they now find themselves in the midst of nature, surrounded by all its causes and effects: at the same time, other individuals with similar characteristics share that experience. In my writings I have spoken about humankind as a unique entity in charge – whether consciously or unconsciously – of a destiny which carries it towards the fulfilment of goals, goals which can be proposed or *pre*-posed. But humankind, which must fulfil its purpose, would not be capable of completing this mission if it did not have the help of the environment in which it finds itself: in the same way, humans also need the help of other humans with whom they inevitably have to relate.

This idea of an interrelationship has acquired grand proportions in the last few decades. Today we cannot carry out any task – real or theoretical – without studying the relationship it has both with itself and its environment. Consequently, systems theory has not only begun to be regarded as a fundamental concept once again, but also a subject that should be studied in its own right, all of which means that this subject is currently evolving. Today we talk not only about systems statics or systems dynamics, but also systems dialectics, systemography and even systemometry. Our very concept of 'information science' is the result of the necessary integration of these hermetic compartments in order to establish interrelations and mutual influences. It is now not possible to study library science as if it were completely separate from archibiology or information science. These three disciplines form a system that can be adapted to the laws of systems theory.

Therefore this chapter will be dedicated to the study of systems theory, the most recent trends within this field and their application to our field of activity: thesaurus theory.

Historical evolution

The idea that the different units, simple or compound, that make up our world in all its manifestations can be considered to be isolated individual entities in interaction is not an idea that was born in this century. In the year 2,500 BCE the work *Tao Te King*, attributed to Lao Tse, had already appeared, in which the principle which says that 'the whole is greater than the sum of its parts' was first mentioned, a principle which entails the study of these parts as belonging to the whole.

In the third century BCE, this idea of interrelationsip became generalised when the concept of the principles of yin and yang appeared, opposite and complementary at the same time. Some examples of this concept might be night and day, light and shade.

In Greece, it was not until the time of Plato and Aristotle that these ideas really became important when the word 'system' was coined, which is derived from *syn* = together, and *stesai* = formal cause.

The application of these ideas, which has led to what today is called systems theory, has experienced many highs and lows during the course of humanity's history. The theory itself is affected by the very principles that it proposes. Since the middle of the twentieth century, these ancient methods and systemic theories have been revived by the likes of Bertalanffy, Ashby, Shannon, Weiner, Rappoport and – more recently – Ouellet, De Rosnay, Rudner, Ervin Laszlo and Rodríguez Delgado, among others (see Figure 5.1).

Figure 5.1 Historic evolution of systems science

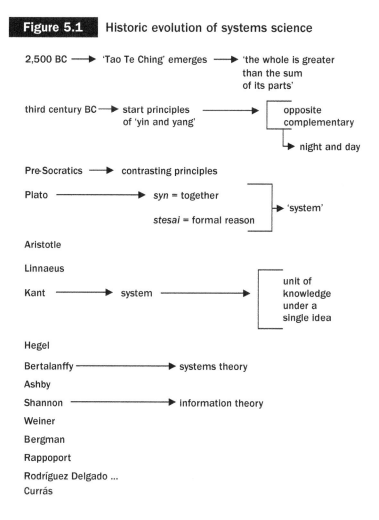

At first, these systems were studied as whole and separate units in interaction with their environment. Nevertheless, they displayed certain behaviours that could not be explained, and so the conclusion was reached that there were some intervening dynamic processes – systems dynamics – that determined the behaviour of these systems. With the aid of systemic simulation, constructing models in which parameters and variables are recorded and give values to the fluxes and refluxes, the behaviour of a system could be predicted. This subject is of great importance in the realisation of economic studies, political developments and market behaviour: it paves the way for operational research, the prospective of advanced studies, inventics, etc.

In the last decades of the twentieth century its study has intensified, leading many people to the conclusion that it might constitute an entirely new way of thinking, *systems thinking*, which would in turn constitute a *systems philosophy*. All of this has paved the way for the formation of a new branch of human knowledge, which is the component of science as a unity which has come to be known as *systems science*.

Approach to systems

We shall start by defining what can be understood by the term system. In the available literature on this subject many different definitions of a system can be found. The most general is that which describes a system as a group of independent entities which have an interrelationship with each other and their surroundings.

Another definition of a system that is appropriate to information science is that of Ellis and Ludwig, who affirm that it is 'a device', procedure or scheme which behaves according to some description, which has the function of operating according to the information and/or energy that it receives, and/or the material that it receives in a time of reference, producing information and/or energy and/or material and information. This leads us to reconsider the nature of information as being a form or expression of energy.

A last meaning of system (that will be outlined here) is that which involves organised groups belonging to different scientific fields which display isomorphic structures and behaviours reducible to a common mathematical treatment into which information science fits in a special way (Currás, 2008).

In order to define systems science I have chosen a definition from the abundant literature that fits in best with the classic concept of this subject: *systems science* – a body of doctrines in accordance with predetermined paradigms which investigates the truth about things (or the world we live in), organising them into structures made up of units in mutual and simultaneous interrelationships with each other and with the environment in which they are found.

A study of *systems taxonomy* leads us to classify systems according to their different characteristics, properties and functions, taking their configuration into account, as well as their complexity, field and many other characteristics (see Figure 5.2).

In a different order of things we could also consider systems in relation to their dimensions, which would mean dividing them into systems.

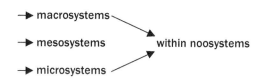

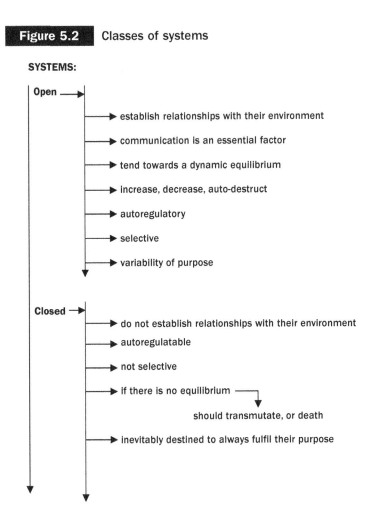

Figure 5.2 Classes of systems

SYSTEMS:

Open
→ establish relationships with their environment
→ communication is an essential factor
→ tend towards a dynamic equilibrium
→ increase, decrease, auto-destruct
→ autoregulatory
→ selective
→ variability of purpose

Closed
→ do not establish relationships with their environment
→ autoregulatable
→ not selective
→ if there is no equilibrium →
should transmutate, or death
→ inevitably destined to always fulfil their purpose

Systems theory applied to the construction of thesauri

It has been said that a system must be situated in an environment from which it receives fluxes or influences which will determine its character. Likewise, we know that each system must have some purpose, which in itself implies a principle of action with a concrete aim. When we wish to create a thesaurus by applying systems theory the task becomes a great deal easier. Consider an institution or an information centre which might need to construct a thesaurus and wants to apply systems theory in order to do so. These needs and the subsequent construction of a thesaurus provide the final aim of the constructed thesaurus itself.

A system will have to be situated in a particular place and concrete space in time. The time can be constant or variable. In the case that we are dealing with, the space will be determined by the institution or information centre that is going to build the thesaurus. The time will be decided by the topicality of the work and will vary, depending on the initial moment when the base thesaurus is constructed and the successive updates and basic maintenance tasks that it is subjected to.

Components

When applying systems theory to the construction of thesauri in a concrete environment and with a concrete aim, the following components should be considered:

- input elements
- output elements
- invariable elements – not manipulable:
  - parameters
- variable (input or output) elements – manipulable:
  - vectors or variables
  - feedback loops.

The *input elements* are those which feed the system, that is they will be determined by the places from which the keywords – terms – are going to be obtained. These will be the documents, vocabularies, glossaries, etc. used in the thesaurus theory, which is the object of the project.

The *output elements* will comprise a single output element, that is to say the thesaurus itself.

The *invariable elements*, which are not manipulable, are those elements which make up the *parameters*, and will consist of keywords converted into terms, descriptors, fixed components of the thesaurus.

The *variable elements* (manipulable) are made up of *vectors*, which are also variable, and will be determined by the input and output vectors, and the feedback loops which are responsible for the evolution of the system.

Here the principal *holon*, which is the basic element for the whole system, will always be the future term component of the thesaurus in question.

Classes of system

A thesaurus is in itself a highly complex system composed of different classes of systems and subsystems, and it is necessary to study and review some of these types of system. For the sake of simplicity, in our context we could consider *the main system*. This will comprise the thesaurus itself, containing all the terms, relationships and influxes between them. It is a highly complex system within which all the corresponding subsystems – also highly complex – are contained.

On the other hand, the *terms* will also form a system, equally complex, whose *parameters* will be made up of the following classes of terms: main terms or descriptors, secondary terms and synonymous terms.

For their part, the *descriptors* will be structured into families composed of headings, generic terms, specific terms and related terms.

We can deduce from all this that a thesaurus as a system is made up of:

- a main system: the thesaurus itself

- a primary subsystem: the terms themselves

- a secondary subsystem: the classes of terms

- a tertiary subsystem: the relationships between terms in hierarchical order

and a whole group of subsystems that will not be discussed here for the sake of a clear and simple general explanation.

In all these systems and subsystems the *variable elements*, the elements which move the system and which can also be called *feedback loops*, necessarily have to be taken into account. In this case, it will be necessary to refer to semantic and syntactic relationships which will determine where the terms will be located.

It could be assumed that the terms are composed of a single word; however, this is not always true. It is therefore necessary to think about the syntactic relationships between the components of compound terms.

A *causal diagram* must then be constructed which features the relevant system (see Figure 5.3). A study of this causal diagram paves the way for the more comprehensive construction of a thesaurus which is more easily assimilated, taking the rest of the components and relevant considerations into account.

The construction of a *flow diagram* will also help in the study of the construction of a thesaurus. Figure 5.4 shows an example of such a flow diagram, in which the direction

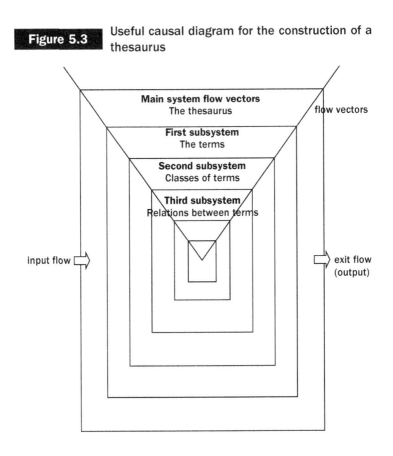

Figure 5.3 Useful causal diagram for the construction of a thesaurus

of action, directed by the feedback loops, can be seen, which in turn indicate the stages that should be successively completed.

All the above has been explained in a brief and simplified way. In the real world, this process is much more laborious and meticulously detailed. Moreover, other subjects that could be seen as being completely separate from the main topic must also be taken into account, such as the computer system used or the intervention of people who contribute words that emerge sporadically in an unusual document.

Figure 5.4 Useful flow diagram for the construction of a thesaurus

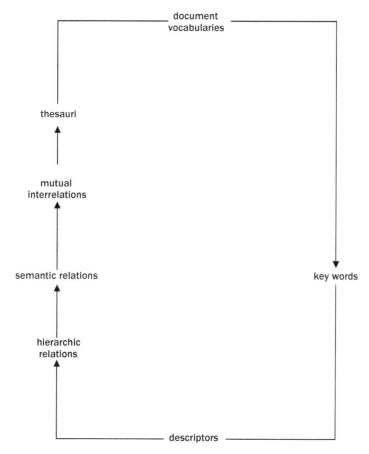

Peculiarities of these systems

The system created for the construction of a thesaurus should be:

- conceptual
- real
- linear
- pragmatic
- complex

- open
- evolutionary
- dynamic
- fluctuating
- approximate.

As with any open system, in order for the system to work, the input flows will have to be more or less continuously constant or periodic; this will ensure that the thesaurus constructed can be influenced by revisions, updates and maintenance which will determine the inclusion or deletion of terms. These operations will affect the positions of the terms involved, and also, therefore, all the relationships between them. Thus a dynamism, fluctuation and evolution of the system, the thesaurus, are achieved.

In these maintenance and update tasks, the input elements – the base documents, vocabularies, glossaries, etc. – can also vary. Likewise, the output elements will also vary, resulting in a remodelled thesaurus.

Working methods

As a conclusion to this chapter, some simple rules for action will be described that can be applied when the use of systems theory is required in the construction of a thesaurus.

The preliminary steps will be determined by familiar questions:

1. The subject of work.
2. The institution that needs to make the thesaurus.
3. The proposed aim – the class of thesaurus to be created:
    - starting elements: documents, vocabularies, etc. that will provide the terms;
    - basic elements: terms – descriptors – to be used;
    - establishment of relationships: between terms.

All this will be carried out following any of the usual methods of thesaurus construction.

When the final and fundamental body of work has been completed, the following elements must be decided on:

- the main system;
- the following subsystems;
- the subsystems that come after that ...

until a simpler configuration system is obtained which will contain a specific holon as a starting element.

The following step will consist of constructing a causal diagram where the majority of the elements that constitute the system will appear. If there are a large number of these elements, it might be advisable to divide the causal diagram into sub-diagrams containing a smaller number of elements which can be integrated later.

The corresponding flow diagram can be constructed more or less simultaneously. If necessary, partial sub-diagrams can also be constructed.

The system will not be complete unless the parameters and variables of the place of action are taken into account. It will be necessary to add elements such as economics, budgets, consumable costs, general costs, potential profit, etc. Human factors should also be taken into account, such as the types of existing employees or their mutual relationships, etc. and other various factors related to working conditions. All in all, everything that affects the institution or centre in question should be taken into account.

With all these elements, partial systems, causal diagrams and flow diagrams are constructed which will be necessary in order for the system to be operative.

Subsequently, the partial systems will be integrated. It is very important that we understand that interrelations are created between the systems when they are integrated and that they can affect or modify the main system as a whole. It is necessary to be very cautious and thoughtful when carrying out these operations.

Once the integrations and appropriate or necessary considerations have been dealt with, the final stage has been reached and our much desired thesaurus will be complete.

Systems theory applied to ontologies and taxonomies

In previous chapters it has been assumed that ontologies and taxonomies are classification systems which have a similar construction to that of a thesaurus. In fact, both ontologies and taxonomies are particular kinds of thesauri. This means that systems theory could be applied to both.

The question is much more complex in this case, since the plurality implied by their multiple purposes must be taken into account.

The main holon, which is the term, is not simple either. Often the terms are made up of short phrases with a complex conceptual content.

The input and output vectors and feedback loops are subject to fluctuations in many cases, with no defined – or foreseeable – periodicity, which increases the complexity of the system.

That is not to say that, due to such complexity, the task of constructing an ontology or a taxonomy using systems theory should not be carried out, but I do want to make clear that it is not a simple task. Nevertheless, it can be extremely useful and worthwhile, when you consider that these are systems in which the elements are related to each other, and take all factors and considerations into account.

The method used will be the same: input and output flows and parameters and vectors will be determined. A causal diagram and a flow diagram will then be made, and the external and internal influences will be determined. Using these methods the desired ontology or taxonomy can be achieved.

Topics for discussion

1. How would you describe a system?

2. Do you think that archibiology can comprise a system?

3. Give an example of a system type.

4. How would you classify a system in which a thesaurus is included?

5. Give a definition of systems theory.

6. Do you agree that the construction of a thesaurus can be done within the framework of systems theory?

7. Do you think that there are any systemic principles that can be applied to multilingual thesauri?

8. Do you believe that everything is actually related to everything else, and that humanity's progress depends on the influences and interactions of its parts with themselves and with each other?

9. How would you apply systems theory to an ontology?

References

Ackoff, R. (2004) 'Systems Thinking and Its Implications for Management'. Contact: *dynamics@sas.upenn.edu*.

Barite Roqueta, M.G. (1999) 'La noción de – categoría – y sus implicaciones en la construcción y evaluación de lenguajes documentales', IV Congreso ISKO-España EOCONSID '99, in M.J. López-Huertas and J.C. Fernández Molina (eds), *Representación y organización del conocimiento en sus distintas perspectivas: su influencia en la recuperación de la información*, 4: 39–45.

Bertalanffy, L. von (1968) *General System Theory. Foundations, Development, Application*. New York: Georges Braziller.

Bertalanffy, L. von (1979) *Perspectiva en la Teoría General de Sistemas*. Madrid: Alianza Universal.

Bliss, H.E. (1929) *Organization of Knowledge and the System of the Sciences*. New York: H.W. Wilson & Co.

Currás, E. (1987) 'Intelligence and communication within the system theory', in B.V. Smith and S. Keenan (eds), *Information, Communication and Technology Transfer*, FID nr. 663, pp. 65–74.

Currás, E. (1987) 'Science as a system of cyclic process of generation processing, accumulation and transfer of scientific information', *Theoretical Problems of Informatics. Place of Information in the Global Problems of the World*. VINITI, ed. FID nr. 659, pp. 10–26.

Currás, E. (1992) 'Information science – information as a dialectic interactive system', Second International ISKO Conference, Madras, 1992, in *Cognitive Paradigms in Knowledge Organization*, Sarada Ranganathan Endowment for Library Science, pp. 419–31; ed. FID, 20 (1) (January 1995): 31–42.

Currás, E. (1992) 'The vertical integration of sciences as a stabilizing factor for mankind', in Rafael Rodríguez Delgado and Bela H. Banathy (eds), *International Systems Science Handbook*. The Samos Seminar by Ioanna Tsivocou. Samos: International Society for Systems.

Currás, E. (1997) 'Enfoque sistémico de la clasificación documental', in María Pinto (ed.), *Manual de Clasificación Documental*. Madrid: Síntesis.

Currás, E. (1999) 'Dialéctica en la organización del conocimiento', *Organ. Conoc. Sist. Inf. Doc.*, 3: 23–43.

Currás, E. (2002) 'Vertical integration of sciences: an approach to a different view of knowledge organization', *Journal of Information Science*, 28 (5): 417–26.

Currás, E. (2008) *Ciencia de la Información bajo postulados sistémicos y sistemáticos*. Madrid: Edición personal.

Fuchs, Ch. (2003) 'Internet as system and environment', *Triple C*, 2, online at: *http.//www.triplec.uti.at*.

Gilchrist, A. (1984) 'Comentario a la Conferencia de P.B. Chekland sobre System and Science, Industry and Innovation', *Journal of Information Science*, 9 (4): 65–74.

Godert, W. and Jaencke, P. (2001) 'Kognitive Ansetze zum Ordnen und Darstellen von Wissen', *2 Tagund der Deutschen ISKO Secktion*. Weilburg, pp. 15–18.

Henning, W. (1966) *Phylogenetic Systematic*. Urbana, IL: University of Illinois Press.

La Teoría de Sistemas y la Ingeniería de Sistemas de la Investigación Científica. Online at: *http://www.concytec .gob.pe/institucional/sistemas.htm*.

Ouellet, A. (1983) *L'évolution creative: Une approche systémique des valeurs*. Québec: Presses de l'Université du Québec.

Quijano, A. (2003) 'Los Sistemas Inquisitivos (inquiring) de Churman y las bibliotecas', *VIII Encuentros Internacionales sobre Sistemas de Información y Documentación*. Zaragoza: IBERSID.

van Gigch, J.P. (2003) *Metadecisions: Rehabilitating Epistemology*, Contemporary Systems Thinking series. New York: C. West Churchman.

Author index

Subject index

Printed and bound by CPI Group (UK) Ltd, Croydon, CR0 4YY

03/10/2024

01040437-0018